ARSENAL
A BACKPASS THROUGH HISTORY

Written by
Michael O'Neill

BOOKS

© Danann Publishing Ltd 2017

First Published by Danann Publishing Ltd 2014

CAT NO: DAN0356

Photography courtesy of The Press Association & Getty Images,
Photoshot, UPPA, Talking Sport, Fotosports

Book layout & design Darren Grice at **Ctrl-d**

Made in EU.
ISBN: 978-1-9997050-4-6

THE CONTENTS

INTRODUCTION

It is impossible to trace the exact origins of what evolved into the riveting sport known as football, the *"beautiful game"*; they are lost somewhere in the mists of memory that swirl around human activity as they may do on an autumn morning at Anfield. So we must indulge in that wonderful pastime, speculation, spiced with some good, calculated guesses.

Whenever football is mentioned, Britain will be part of the conversation before long, so it is fitting that Britain has its part in the ancient folklore of the origins of the sport.

Local legends in both Chester and Kingston-on-Thames tell us that a game was played in those towns in which the amputated head of a defeated Danish prince or ruffian, which probably came to the same thing, was kicked around. That seems to be a good starting point; considering the curses from the terraces that wish a similar fate would befall the top goal-scorers of opposing teams in the present-day game. In Derbyshire they would have us believe that Anglo-Saxon victory celebrations against the Romans brought on the desire to kick something else, as kicking the Romans had been such fun.

Long before that, written evidence supports the claim that the Romans and Greeks were instrumental in the game's birth. They played many ball games as the Roman writer Cicero testified. One unfortunate man was killed whilst having a shave, he wrote, when a ball came hurtling into the barber's shop where he was sitting. The Romans used ball games for more serious reasons, too. They were considered a good way to sharpen a soldier's reactions and spirit for battle.

The Chinese, inventive as they have always been, seem to have been ahead of the game as well. A form of football was played in the third and second centuries BC. during the Han dynasty, when people were already rushing around and kicking leather balls into a small net or through a hole in a piece of silk cloth stretched between two poles. It was probably played for the emperor's amusement. There is no record of what happened if he got bored and relegation would not have been much fun back then. The game, as played by Chinese aristocrats, was known as t'su chu. But the Aztecs, Persians, Vikings and Japanese all had some form of ball game for entertainment. Luckily not against one another.

It was the English peasants, however, who were responsible for the increasing popularity of the game sometime around the 9th century AD. This old football game was a real free-for-all and participants were allowed to bite, punch, stab and gouge as well as kick. Not much has changed in a thousand years after all. The ball had to be taken to a certain spot and this game proved to be so popular that fields would be overflowing with eager sports fans. As you can imagine, it often got wildly out of hand. Archers would even sneak away from archery practice to watch.

Medieval England was undoubtedly the place where football began its unstoppable campaign. There is an account of a match played in 1280. It took place in Northumberland near Ashington. It is also the first report of a player being killed when he ran onto the dagger worn by an opposing player. There is no report as to whether the dagger was in or out of the sheath at the time!

Incidents of violence became so frequent, in fact, that in 1365 King Edward the Third banned the game altogether. The ban was also an attempt to keep his archers at their practice (yes, they were still sneaking away from work) as their skills were sorely needed following the outbreak of the black plague that had decimated the population of the country. King James the First of Scotland was very upset with the ruckus the ball game caused and went even further, declaring in 1424 that *"Na man play at the Fute-ball"*. Perhaps his team kept losing.

So by medieval times Britain was already in the grip of football fever.

Moving along another half century and dribbling and areas marked out for the game had come into existence as the manuscript collection of the miracles of King Henry VI of England testifies:

". . . is called by some the foot-ball game. It is one in which young men, in country sport, propel a huge ball not by throwing it into the air but by striking it and rolling it along the ground and that not with their hands but with their feet . . ".

King Henry VIII reputedly bought the first pair of football boots in 1526, and football had become much more organised by then. By 1581 English schools were providing reports of *"parties"* or *"sides"*, *"judges over the parties"* and *"training masters"*. But although the violence had lessened it still raised its head. In 1595 a document stated: *"Gunter's son and ye Gregorys fell together . . . at football. Old Gunter drew his dagger and both broke their heads, and they died both within a fortnight after".*

By the 1600s, football was an established and increasingly popular part of British life and references to it had found their way into the literature of the day. In 1608, Shakespeare had King Lear say, *"Nor tripped neither, you base football player".* This was the first time "football" had been spelt in the modern manner. *" . . . lusty shepherds try their force at football, care of victory . . . They ply their feet, and still the restless ball, toss'd to and fro, is urged by them all".* That was the English Poet Edmund Waller (c.1624). *"The streete (in London) being full of footballs".* That was the famous diarist Samuel Pepys in 1665.

In Manchester in 1608 the local authorities complained that: *"With the ffotebale . . . there hath beene great disorder in our towne of Manchester we are told, and glasse windowes broken . . . by a companie of lewd and disordered persons using that unlawful exercise of playing with the ffotebale in ye streets of the said towne . . ".*

Must have been visiting fans . . .

Football had come so far by 1660 that a book was written about it, the first objective study of the game in England. The author was Francis Willoughby and he called his work the Book of Sports. It refers to goals and pitches, (goalkeeping had already been established by this time) to scoring and selecting teams and striking balls through goals. There is also a basic sketch of a football pitch and mention that a rule had been introduced so that players could not strike their opponent higher than the ball otherwise they often *" . . . break one another's shins when two meet and strike together against the ball".*

Even though football was often outlawed in many areas of the country, with violators threatened with imprisonment, it remained popular even amongst aristocrats. *"Lord Willoughby . . . with so many of their servants . . . play'd a match at foot-ball against such a number of Countrymen, where my Lord of Sunderland being busy about the ball, got a bruise in the breast".*

Football was really put on the map in 1681 when King Charles II of England attended a game between the Royal Household and George Monck, 1st Duke of Albemarle's servants. Football was here to stay.

In the 1800s, when the working man's day lasted twelve hours or more and six days a week, the only men who had enough leisure to indulge in football were the wealthy. Their sons at private schools were encouraged to play to develop a competitive spirit and keep themselves fit and so the rules developed that produced the game as we know it today. Nonetheless, there were a variety of rules regulating the matches so in 1848 Mr. H. de Winton and Mr. J. C. Thring called a meeting at Cambridge University with twelve representatives from other schools; their eight-hour discussions produced the first set of modern rules, the Cambridge rules.

So in the truth, mankind has probably been throwing and kicking anything from monkey heads to coconuts and turnips since before he could walk upright. But there are at least 3,000 years of history behind the football match of today.

The millennia have passed and football, soccer, has become one of the most exciting mass entertainments of all time.

THE FOOTBALL LEAGUE

C lubs dedicated solely to the sport of football were formed regularly throughout the 18th century. The London Gymnastic Society was one of the first created in the 1850s. The first club to be referred to as a club was the *"Foot-Ball Club of Edinburgh"* in Scotland in the period 1821 to 1824. Great Leicestershire Cricket and Football Club existed in 1840. The staff of Guy's Hospital in London formed Guys Hospital Football Club in 1843 which claims to be the oldest known football club, whilst Sheffield Football Club founded in 1857, is the oldest club documented as not being affiliated to a school, university or other institution. The oldest club still playing association football is Cambridge University Association Football Club.

Soon, club names that are recognisable to fans today were appearing; Bolton Wanderers (1874), Aston Villa (1874), Queen's Park (1867), Sheffield Wednesday (1867); and of course there was a certain Newton Heath LYR Football Club which was formed by railway workers in 1878. What would they say today about the extraordinary club they started?

The time had come to try and make a set of rules that would be adhered to by all the clubs. In 1862, thirteen London clubs met and hammered out regulations to govern the sport. This led to the formation of the Football Association in 1863 to oversee regulations for the sport.

No history of football would be complete if the name of Ebenezer Cobb Morely was not mentioned. He was a central figure in bringing the Football Association into being. He was a player himself and a founding member of the Football Association. As captain of his team, the Barnes Club, he proposed a governing body for the sport and so the meeting of the thirteen London clubs came about. From 1863-1866 he was the FA's first secretary and from 1867-1874 its second president. He drafted the *"London Rules"* at his home in Barnes in London.

Another event must be mentioned here: the first official, international game between England and Scotland took place in November 1872 on the West of Scotland cricket ground in Partick, Scotland. 4,000 spectators watched a 0-0 draw although the Scots had a goal disallowed. The very first game had taken place on the 5th March 1870 at the Oval cricket ground in London.

Most of the men playing in the teams at the time were amateurs, although betting had long been a feature of the sport. On the 18th July 1885 it was finally decided that football could become a professional sport. But clubs were still setting their own fixture dates and the whole structure was chaotic. Now was the moment for another man to step into the limelight, Mr. William McGregor, a director of Aston villa Football Club and to make his mark on history.

It was the 2nd March 1888. McGregor wrote to the committees of several football clubs to propose that a league competition would guarantee a certain number of fixtures and bring some order into the confusion that then existed. In Anderson's Hotel in London on the 23rd

Original Handwritten Rules 1863

March 1888, on the eve of the FA Cup Final, a meeting was held to discuss the proposal. Manchester was once again in the headlines when on the 17th April at the Royal Hotel, a final meeting created the Football League.

On the 8th September 1888, twelve clubs Accrington, Aston Villa, Blackburn Rovers, Derby County, Everton, Notts County, Preston North End, Stoke, FC., West Bromwich Albion and Wolverhampton Wanderers, sent their players out onto the turf for the first games in the new football league season.

Only once the season was underway was it decided that clubs would play against one another twice, once at home and once away, with two points awarded for a win and one for a draw. For the record, Preston won the first league title without losing a single game and won the FA Cup Final, too, the first league-FA Cup double.

Three clubs dominated during those first exciting years; Preston North End, Aston Villa and Sunderland; for fourteen seasons only three other clubs would win league titles; Everton, Sheffield United and Liverpool.

In 1892 the league expanded with the addition of a new Second Division. Liverpool, Arsenal and Newcastle United were now on the scene and a new name had been added to the First Division. A club with a glorious future had made its first steps to the top. Fourteen years had passed since they had first formed but now Newton Heath had arrived in the First Division.

Six years later, 1898, the number of clubs in each league had increased to eighteen and automatic promotion and relegation for two clubs was introduced the same year.

The Third Division was only added after WWI in 1921. By then another host of names that would later become legendary, including Tottenham Hotspur, Chelsea and Fulham, had been added to divisions that by 1905 had been boosted in numbers to 20 clubs in each. There were two third divisions in fact, the Third Division North and the Third Division South. Newton Heath by that time had become Manchester United having changed their name and moved to Old Trafford in 1902.

With the coming of WWII, the league was suspended for seven seasons. In 1950 there were 24 clubs in each of the two third divisions so there were now 92 league clubs. The third division clubs were amalgamated into a single division abolishing regionalisation and the

Fourth Division was added in 1958. Four clubs could be promoted and relegated in the lower two divisions. In divisions one and two until 1974, two clubs made the climb or fell; the number was increased to three that same year.

The league now entered a period of calm with only minor changes such as altering the points system, three instead of two for a win introduced in 1981, and goal differences being taken into account. There was one enormous change ahead, however.

On May 27th 1992 the Premier League was formed. All First Division clubs resigned together from the Football League, which now operated with three divisions. The old system of interaction between the leagues, however, did not change but 104 years of tradition were over. The elite clubs were now, literally, in a league of their own. Money had tempted the top clubs and lucrative television rights deals beckoned them. The deal will soon be worth three billion pounds.

This wealth, of course, makes it almost impossible for a promoted club to compete with the big boys in the first season after promotion, and relegation often follows immediately. But the rewards for the successful are enormous with British Premier League clubs amongst the richest in the world and able to buy in players to make the....

....terraces on a Saturday afternoon one of the most thrilling places to be.

7

William McGregor regarded as the founder of the Football League

IN THE BEGINNING

Arsenal FC came into being through the drive and dream of one young, homesick man. Yet When David Danskin moved from Scotland to Woolwich in 1885, he had more pressing matters on his mind than football. He needed a job. He had escaped the restrictions of life as an apprentice fitter in Kirkcaldy in Scotland for a better life in London, and at the age of 22, he began work at the Woolwich Arsenal Munitions Factory in Dial Square. Once the problem of employment was solved however, David realised that he had moved to an area that was only interested in tennis and rugby. The young Scot was not about to anglicise himself that much; he had played for Kirkcaldy Wanderers, he missed his football. So much, in fact, that he gathered two friends about him that were also fans of the game, and between the three of them, they set about realising a modest dream, the dream of creating a football team.

Before long a team had been put together from the men in the factory; a whip-round enabled them to buy a football, and a name that would resound with football glory was born in the Royal Oak pub on the 1st December 1886; Dial Square FC.

Well ... that's what history might have recorded.

Dial Square was the location of the munitions factory workshop where the lads worked — the name derived from the sundial above the workshop door — and it was the name they gave to their first team, which ran out onto a field on the Isle of Dogs in East London on the 11th December 1886, wearing kit that the lads had gathered from wherever they could find it. The historic first match, against Eastern Wanderers, more of a mud bath than a football game by all accounts, gave Dial Square a 6-0 victory, although there was some dispute about that score … of course! (There are also disputes about the line up that day: writer Bernard Joy mentioned that the line up was: Danskin, Morris, Beardsley, Bee, Porteous, Moy, Duggan, Wolfe, Gregory, Smith, Whitehead. Robert Thompson insisted that he had played and, apparently, Wells had played, too, not Morris or Duggan. Thompson also claimed the first goal. To muddy the picture a little more, Beardsley was found to have been in the FA Cup fixture for Nottingham Forest on the same day. And to make the whole picture wobble, all the facts surrounding that first match have been questioned. The facts, therefore, might not be facts; the circumstances are unclear, and whilst they remain so, the description just given is probably as near to the truth as any.

Danskin must have been well pleased, but he wanted to move his humble venture forwards, and quickly. There were three problems he needed to solve; shirts, a pitch and a new name. Two of the Dial Square players, Fred Beardsley and Morris Bates had played for Nottingham Forest before taking up jobs at Woolwich. It was goalkeeper Beardsley who was responsible for solving the first problem. He returned from a visit to his old club one day with an armful of red shirts and another ball. Many of the players met up in The Royal Oak to discuss progress and to decide on a name for the club. Some argued to retain the old name, but when left-winger Thompson mentioned that everyone had heard the name, Royal Arsenal, but few had heard of Dial Square, the new club had found a name. It was the 25th December 1886 … a date which proves how important Arsenal had already become to the men involved. Royal Arsenal was born on Christmas day! Now, the legend could unfold.

The final problem was solved with the choice of Plumstead Common as the pitch for the new club's first match. It was also used by the Royal Artillery, and the surface was not only stony, it had been churned up. Still, the ever-enterprising Beardsley had got hold of goalposts, and they were brought up from his back garden for the great match on the 8th January 1887. The dressing room was The Star Inn pub. It appears that the team still answered to the name of Dial Square in their first outings of 1887. But the start was as good as it could be for the men in red, a 6-1 win against Erith. And what a terrific season it proved to be. Although there was defeat, 4-0 against Millwall Rovers on the 5th February 1887 — which was unfortunate because this was the first time the had club played under its new name, Royal Arsenal — there was also a whopping 11-0 defeat of Alexandra United to celebrate. Arsenal was already a name to be reckoned with, and there was increased interest in the club.

1887 was an historic year for another reason; two great rivals clashed for the first time. Arsenal's first game against Tottenham Hotspur was a friendly that took place on the 19th November that year, on Tottenham Marshes. It ended with a 2-1 defeat for Arsenal, with Beardsley emerging as the hero for preventing an even higher score line for Tottenham; bad light ended the game after 75 minutes. Arsenal would have to wait for nearly ten years to get revenge.

The search for a permanent ground went on into the next year, 1888, and the years that followed. The Sportsman Ground at Plumstead Marshes was tried out, but rain turned it into a field of mud. The next move was to Manor Field, close to Plumstead Station, and there, over the next two years, Royal Arsenal began to forge their reputation, closing their first season with just two losses.

Arsenal were rising stars from the start, fortunate because the Empire needed munitions to send to the colonies, and the munitions factory jobs could be used by the club to tempt players that it wanted in the team. Soon, they were semi-finalists in the London Senior Cup, in 1889, but they went down to Clapton, 2-0. There were impressive wins in the 1889-90 FA Cup run; 11-0 against Lyndhurst and 5-2 against Crusaders, although they didn't reach the final. But 1890 was still a memorable year; they won the Kent Senior Cup, 3-0, against Thanet, the London Charity Cup, 3-1, against Old Westminster and the Kent Junior Cup. The London Senior Cup was in their hands in 1891 after they defeated St Bartholomew's Hospital 6-0. Here was a team to be reckoned with.

By now they were in need of a better, and above all, a bigger ground, so in 1890, another move took place. Their new home was the Invicta Ground, not far from Plumstead High Street. Still an amateur club with crowds of some 1,000 for their matches, Royal Arsenal set off into a future that would see great changes within the year. In a mighty friendly at the new ground on Easter Monday 1891, Royal Arsenal played a home match against Heart of Midlothian, the Scottish champions. 12,000 fans turned up to watch. With the score 1-1 at half time, the London men were holding their own. But the second half did the damage, and the visitors went home with a 5-1 win under their belts.

Arsenal stayed at the Invicta for the next two years

1891 was to prove a turning point for the ambitious club. That was the year that Derby County FC attempted to poach two Arsenal players following an FA Cup match between the two sides. To add insult to injury, Arsenal lost 2-1, but Derby's actions made Danskin and fellow founding member Jack Humble aware that their efforts were doomed to failure if they could not prevent their best players being siphoned off, especially to the professional northern clubs.

At the club's AGM that year, Humble put forward the proposal that the team should become a professional side, although the club should not, in his opinion, become a limited company. Arsenal had been run by working men, *"… and it is"*, he said, *"… my ambition to see it carried on by them"*. The decision was taken. It was a brave one because the southern

John Wilkinson Humble

amateur leagues were greatly suspicious of the professional northern leagues. Would any of the London clubs join Arsenal and incur the wrath of the London FA? It turned out that they would not, and Arsenal found itself expelled from the London FA and banned from its competitions. In the only competition they could play in, the FA Cup, Arsenal were walloped in 1892, 5-1 by Small Heath, now Birmingham City. In 1893, after a promising run of four games, they were well and truly whacked by Sunderland, 6-0. The omens were not good.

That same meeting in 1891 had determined that the club would now be known as Woolwich Arsenal. The new club was to face almost two years of immense difficulties and might well have vanished from the face of the football world. When Arsenal attempted to start a professional Southern League with 12 other London clubs in 1892, the London FA threatened to expel those clubs, too, and the scheme collapsed, leaving Arsenal a lonely voice in the wilderness with no local fixtures.

Needs must when the devil drives, so the club applied to join the Football League. It was a good time to apply for membership because the league had decided to expand the Second Division from 12 to 15 clubs. In fact, five new clubs entered the League that year because Bootle and Accrington, who had been demoted, decided not to continue playing in the League; a fatal decision for them, but for Middlesborough, Newcastle, Liverpool, Rotherham and Woolwich Arsenal, the door to the future had been opened. Three of the greatest clubs in the history of English football had arrived in the Second Division, and Arsenal also made history because they were the first southern club to be elected to the Football League.

As always, success brought problems; the owner of the Invicta ground asked for an increase in rent from £250 to £300 per year. The men at Arsenal were not exactly rolling in cash, so they refused to pay. Yet with the help of their supporters they managed to buy their old ground, the Manor Ground, and got to work to prepare for a future which, had they known what was in store,

would have made David Danskin and

Jack Humble burst with pride.

Arsenal squad 1888

THE EARLY YEARS

Cash flow, the eternal problem; it raised its head at Arsenal, too, and during the summer of 1893, the club became a limited company after all. But as most of the shares went to workers from the munitions factory, the spirit of the club that Humble had wished to see retained, was indeed undiminished.

The great day arrived; the 2nd of September 1893. Woolwich Arsenal ran out against Newcastle United for their first match, at home, in Division Two. The result, a 2-2 draw, was symbolic, unfortunately, because for the next ten years, Arsenal remained a team unable to lift itself out of the Second Division. They finished 9th out of 15 at the end of their first season, which wasn't wonderful, but not terrible, and there would be improvement. There were memorable wins for fans to cheer during that first season; 12-0 against Ashford United in the FA Cup on October 14th, 6-0 against Northwich Victoria, 6-3 against Middlesborough Iron in the league. But there were equally memorable losses against fellow newcomers; 6-0 against Newcastle United, 5-0 against Liverpool.

The club managed to crawl up the league over the next two years to finish 8th in 1895 (with two wins against Newcastle United, 4-2 away and 3-2 at home; sweet revenge for the previous season's defeats), and then 7th in the 1895-96 season. Forwards Peter Mortimer and Henry Boyd kept the goals coming for the 'Reds' for those two seasons, claiming 23 and 22 apiece. Arsenal's first international player, the 24-stone half-back and captain, Welshman Caesar Augustus Llewelyn Jenkyns, moved onto Newton Heath, later Manchester United, after just one season with the Reds. Newton Heath had thrashed Arsenal 5-1 in November 1895, which showed that Arsenal still had a lot to do to catch up with the big boys. A 6-1 defeat against Burnley in the FA Cup in 1896 only confirmed what the Arsenal men already knew, and a terrible accident to one of the players that year seemed indicative of the malaise afflicting the club. Joseph Powell was Arsenal's right-back and captain. In a game against Kettering Town on the 23rd November 1896, Powell fell badly and broke his arm. Blood poisoning set in and he contracted tetanus. Although the arm was amputated, Powell died less than one week later; he was just 26 years of age.

It was decided to appoint a secretary-manager for the club and try to turn the team's fortunes around. The first appointee was T. B. Mitchell, soon replaced by George Elcoat. Otherwise nothing much changed; the team managed 10th, 5th and 7th for the next three seasons.

Then, in 1899 Harry Bradshaw arrived as secretary-manager. He would bring to Arsenal a heady taste of success for the first time. The results of his stewardship were not immediate but they were steady. Two Jimmys, Jackson and Ashcroft arrived to bolster the team and over the next three seasons, Arsenal began to increase in power and moved up the table to finish 3rd in 1902-03 season. They were above Manchester United and only three points short of the second placed Small Heath. Three away losses in December 1902 had put them on the back foot. But goals were coming thick and fast from inside forward Tim Coleman, who smacked in 19 that season, and William Henry Gooing who had scored 10 the season before and in 1903 had scored another 18. The fans began to dream about what had seemed impossible; promotion.

With the improved performance came higher gate receipts so it was with high hopes that the fans and players came together for the first match of the 1903-04 season. Gooing and Coleman were in the front row again on the 5th September 1903 for the match against Blackpool at home and the Reds got off to a flying start for the season with 3-0 victory. As the wins began to pile up, they won the first eight games, (twice hitting home 8 goals; against Burton United and Leicester City) and began another five-match undefeated run in February 1904. The final game against Port Vale was a draw and it was enough to make the dream come true. Arsenal were one point clear of third-placed Manchester United and just one point behind the leaders, Preston North End. With 59 points, the Reds were second in the table and were promoted to the First Division. Gooing and Coleman had again struck gold with 19 and 23 goals apiece, but the top goalscorer that wonderful season was Irishman Thomas Shanks. The inside-left hammered in 25 goals as Arsenal chased for the grand prize.

To everyone's dismay, Bradshaw left the club at the end of the season to manage Fulham. It was the start of fluctuating fortunes both on and off the pitch for the club. Bradshaw was succeeded by Phil Kelso who for the next five years, steered the team through a series of see-saw performances which led to a steady decline, despite two brief rallies; 10th, 12th, 7th, 14th, 6th and 18th positions; club finances took a battering as a result, not helped by the generally lower crowd attendances caused by Arsenal's relative isolation from its northern rivals. The best season during this uncertain period, was 1908-09 when they finished 6th with Tom Fitchie the highest scorer with just 10 goals. But they were still 15 points adrift of leaders Newcastle United on 53. This was the closest the team would get to glory before disaster struck; first the club and then the world.

In 1910 Arsenal was virtually bankrupt and went into voluntary liquidation. The new manager, George Morrell who had joined the club in 1908, was faced with every manager's nightmare; he was forced to sell his best players. To no avail. The inevitable dip in performance followed and after winning just two matches out of 14 at the beginning of the season, Arsenal ended in 18th place. None of the strikers had netted more than 5 goals. They escaped relegation by two points. The club was put up for sale in 1910.

Now a man stepped into the limelight at Arsenal, who was to set the scene for the future course of the club for many years to come. Henry Norris.

Norris was a wealthy football fanatic who was already chairman of Fulham FC when he became a majority shareholder at Arsenal. His plan was to amalgamate the two clubs to form a super club, and Craven Cottage would be the home ground for the new team. The League rejected the proposal and added that Norris had given rise to a conflict of interests with his chairmanship of two clubs. Norris made a decision that would impact enormously on the Reds. He decided to champion Arsenal's cause.

He must have wondered what he had done when Arsenal came 10th for two seasons in a row and then plummeted to 20th in the 1912-13 season; with that, they were back in the Second Division; and had just £19 in funds to show for their efforts. It was the worst record for a club in Division One at the time.

But Norris had already been actively working to solve the problem. The Manor Ground flooded regularly reducing a match to nothing more than a 'mud revel' as one paper reported. If Arsenal were to become a major

force in football this could not go on. Norris had decided to place the club closer to the centre of London and was looking for a site for a new ground that would be easily accessible by public transport. He chose Islington and soon had land owned by St. John College of Divinity in his sights. Norris was a formidable negotiator, and despite vehement opposition from Chelsea, Tottenham and Clapton, and not least from the Arsenal fan base at Woolwich, a £20,000 lease acquired in March 1913 secured Arsenal's new home at Highbury, a place that became a Mecca for Arsenal fans; it was to host some of the most exciting football ever played in England.

With a draw on April 26th 1913, Arsenal said goodbye to the Manor Ground. One era had come to end. Another, more glamorous, was about to begin.

Gavin Crawford Played 1891—1898

in the first match of the season, which gave the new ground a favourable baptism. Indeed, The Arsenal won the first three matches, as they did the last two of the season. In between, lay a run of 14 games with just two defeats, and the Reds were challenging for the top places. But they would come to rue the two home defeats against Bury and Huddersfield Town, because they were beaten to the promotion place by Bradford Park Avenue on goal difference with 49 points. Disappointing, but the new season would certainly bring fans much to cheer about.

It did … and it didn't.

Arsenal were reputed to be paying a huge rental fee to Islington Borough Council and their finances remained in a parlous state. Under those circumstances it was impossible to buy new talented players to help them make the leap to greatness.

And by the start of the 1914-15 season, the players thoughts and indeed their fans thoughts, were across the English Channel with the men fighting for their lives and France's freedom, for on August the 4th 1914, war against Germany had been declared. On the same day that Arsenal ran onto the field to play Wolverhampton Wanderers, the 5th September 1914, British soldiers had begun fighting the Battle of the Marne.

The war was not over by Christmas as everyone had confidently predicted. As the weeks passed, players and spectators donned army kit, left Highbury far behind, and joined tens of thousands who were being sent to the front lines in the new year to fight on the killing fields of France. They were volunteers; conscription did not begin until 1916.

Two 'Football Battalions', the 17th and 23rd Battalions of the Middlesex Regiment (1st and 2nd Football Battalions), the 'Die-Hards', had been formed by William Joynson-Hick, MP for Brentford, in December 1914. Many of the men, of course, never returned from the battlefields of France. Nine Bradford City players lost their lives. More than 8,000 officers and men went with the Football Battalions into some of the hardest battles of the war. The soldiers were former players from many of the clubs. Donald Bell, a defender with Bradford City, and Bernard Vann, a centre-forward at Derby County, both won the Victoria cross for exceptional bravery. Neither survived the war. Chelsea's Vivian Woodward was badly injured in the thigh by a German hand grenade. He was sent

When the 1913-14 season began, and now reincarnated as 'The Arsenal', the Reds were ensconced in their new home at Highbury Stadium. Norris had shown his worth as a businessman and raised new investment in the club. Using his myriad contacts, he had also secured the services of Archibald Leitch, an engineer and architect who was making a name for himself constructing football stadia. One of these was Manchester United's Old Trafford. There was feverish activity to get the ground ready for the new season with Norris wisely using local contractors for the work. So with turnstiles, a grandstand and terraces partly built, (but no changing rooms), 20,000 people turned up at Highbury, spilling onto the North Terrace, known as the Laundry End, and the west terrace known as Spion Kop, to watch a 2-1 win against Leicester Fosse

Caesar Jenkyns Played 1895—1896

back to England, and although he returned to the front in August 1916, he managed to survive the war.

Charlie Buchan was an England international who played for Sunderland from 1911 — 1925. He had also been a youngster at Arsenal, and later returned to the club. Buchan enlisted in the Sherwood Foresters in 1915 and was awarded the Military Medal. He rose to become a second lieutenant.

The football season continued into 1915, but under a very heavy cloud. Attendances dropped, and the club's finances fell with them.

Arsenal seemed to be heading for promotion at least, but from the middle of February they lost seven out of nine matches and came home 5th; but it all meant little under the circumstances. Except that, although no one knew it at the time, Arsenal would never play in the Second Division again.

There were calls for football to be suspended for the duration of the conflict, and the League responded.

The clubs engaged in regional league competitions and friendly matches for the remainder of the war years.

Woolwich Arsenal v Newcastle United, **April 1906**

15

BETWEEN THE WARS

In 1919 the league clubs opened their gates for professional league football once more. The minimum wage was now £10 per week, but later it was reduced to £8.00; £6.00 during the closed season.

Arsenal, who should have been playing Second Division football in 1919, found themselves instead lining up against first division Newcastle United on August the 30th. How had that happened? Arsenal had finished 5th in 1915; Wolves and Barnsley had finished above them in the table. There were two extra places to be allocated in the First Division that year, yet Tottenham, who had been last in 1915, found themselves in Division Two, whilst Chelsea, who had finished second from bottom, were kept in the division; Arsenal moved into the remaining

place. Norris had been wheeling and dealing like a dervish, it seems, in what was described as the 'dodgiest' scam that had ever taken place in English football. Unsurprisingly, relations between Spurs and the Reds reached rock bottom. Incidentally, Spurs were back up in the First Division the following season, and the confrontations with Arsenal on the field were not pretty to behold!

As a consolation, Spurs had their revenge. It came in the form of Arsenal's mediocre form for most of the next ten years, including some heart-stopping brushes with demotion. Spurs, on the other hand, could soon boast of having the largest number of spectators in the area.

Norris brought Leslie Knighton to Arsenal, as their manager. There

↑ **Arsenal football team** 1927

were ominous signs during that first post-war season that all was not going as planned, even though 10th place at the end of the 1919-20 season was commendable enough. Top goalscorer, inside-forward Henry Albert White, did his best with 15 goals. But nine games with just one win was not exactly inspiring. Nor was another run of five losses in six games.

Yet the next season, Arsenal finished ninth and hope still had its place amongst the Reds' supporters. Then everything went wrong.

For the start of the 1921-22 season The Gunners could be optimistic. That optimism vanished when only one win peeped out amongst the first seven games. Following a win against Everton, 1-0, they had managed just 5 points in eight games. They then lost four games in a row. In February 1922 they delivered another run of 5 games without a point. Fortunately, again with the help of Henry Albert White, who thumped 19 goals into the net, they rallied to lose just two games out of the final eleven and rolled home in 17th place, but only five points clear of relegated Bradford. It had been a near miss.

1922 was the year that the club adopted a new crest. Royal Arsenal's first crest introduced in 1888, showed three cannon pointing northwards. Now, it portrayed a single cannon, and alongside this was inscribed the name, The Gunners. This crest was replaced in 1925, when the cannon barrel became slimmer and pointed westward.

The Gunners had been taught a lesson. Weak defending had almost doomed them. The effects of the shock lasted through the 1922-23 season, when Arsenal were 11th at the close, before they dropped like a stone, first to 19th position the following season and then to 20th in 1924-25. Norris was bitterly disappointed. His vision had been of an Arsenal team riding high alongside the football greats. Knighton had failed to deliver; Norris took action and the manager was sacked.

By this time, it was not only the Arsenal club that was in trouble; Norris had overreached himself and his business dealings were becoming ever more suspect; there was personal trouble ahead. But in 1925 Norris was to earn the undying gratitude of the Arsenal fans, whose loyalty had been so sorely tested by their team over the past years. Norris appointed a man to be Knighton's successor, who was to lift the club to peaks of performance that had hitherto only been dreamed of. That man was Herbert Chapman. His arrival at Highbury heralded nothing less than a football revolution; the Arsenal team were to be the powerhouse of that

extraordinary era.

Chapman had won the FA Cup, and the First Division title twice in four years as manager of Huddersfield Town, so his arrival in the summer of 1925 to take up the reigns of the team that Huddersfield had walloped 5-0 in February of that year, was a magnificent coup for Norris and the club. And Chapman had applied for the job himself. Of course, the salary of £2,000 per year was an incentive; it was double what he had been earning up until then. But the new man was ambitious both for himself and the club, whose potential, in his eyes, was enormous. He was proved to be absolutely right, even though it took some time for the proof to show itself brightly. He had told Norris that it would take five years to get to the top, but he insisted that they would get there.

17

Herbert Chapman

The new offside rule, which required the presence of just two players of the defending side between an attacking player and the opposition goal, had come into force that year, and Chapman adopted the 3-4-3 formation advocated by Buchan, to take advantage of the rule. The decision to employ a centre-half 'stopper' and a midfield link man was to take the team into a new and glorious era.

But the new manager had a flood of ideas that he wanted to put into practice. One of astute observations that he passed onto his players was that the best time to score was immediately after an attack because the opposition would then be strung out over the field. Chapman was also a disciplinarian, a no-nonsense man who sacked trainer George Hardy on the spot that season, for usurping Chapman's role, as he saw it, by yelling instructions to the team from the sidelines. Another of Chapman's innovations was the weekly team meeting with input welcomed from all sides. Amongst a plethora of his other ideas that were, initially, thwarted by the FA, were; numbers on the players' shirts; a 45-minute clock at the Highbury ground; floodlit midweek matches (although Chapman did have floodlights installed at Highbury for use on training days), and two officials to verify that a ball had crossed the goal line. He even took on the mighty London Electric
Railway Company and managed to have the underground station at Gillespie Road renamed, Arsenal, an event that took place on November 5th 1932.

Hopes were high, understandably, when the Gunners' first match under their new manager took place on the 29th August 1925. It was a home fixture against local rivals Tottenham Hotspur and 50,000 fans turned up to witness the derby. No one could have been blamed for missing the fact that a new world was opening up for Arsenal that day; Tottenham won the game 1-0 despite the presence of the magnificent Charlie Buchan, making his debut for the club. 'The master mind of a great thinker', was one journalist's observation on Buchan after the match. There was excitement mingled with the disappointment.

And the excitement was justified; there followed 19 games and only three losses, although one of those was an horrific 7-0 thrashing by Newcastle United. But a 6-1 win against Bury and a 5-0 hammering of Cardiff City gave the fans more than enough to cheer about. Between them, inside-forward Charlie Buchan and inside-right James Brain

1927 **FA Cup Final Cardiff City v Arsenal**

had left the club, and it seemed symbolic that Brain's score dropped to 0 in six appearances. Amongst the slithering in the league during those years, there had been an historic first Cup Final for The Gunners in 1927, but ironically, it was a misunderstanding between Buchan and Brain resulting in a missed goal opportunity that allowed Cardiff City to bring the cup home to Wales with a 1-0 win, the first time the cup had left England.

Chapman had not been idle, however, during those years of drought. He had been scouting for new talent to build the team he wanted and had acquired names that were soon to propel the Gunners forward with wonderful football. He even recruited from non-league sides, which was not usual at the time. One such young man was Eddie Hapgood of Kettering Town; £750 brought him to London. Alex James was the kind of inspirational player that Chapman wanted at Highbury; he arrived in 1929. David Jack had already come from Bolton in 1928, and Cliff 'Boy' Bastin came in 1929, a player with razor-sharp intelligence, who exactly fitted in with Chapman's vision.

The FA Cup run of that season had been a glowing success that brought the club into the final for the second time, on this occasion against Huddersfield, a game that was heavy with significance. James was the hero of the day, scoring after 17 minutes and setting up Lambert's winning goal with a pinpoint pass through the centre of the field. Arsenal had won their first FA Cup in brilliant style.

By the time Aston Villa's fourth goal went in against Arsenal sending them down to a 4-2 defeat in the final league match of the 1929-30 season, something extraordinary had happened, and the Gunners would go hurtling into a glittering new decade, ready for the big challenges. Who would have dared to believe that for 7 of the next 9 years, titles, and silverware would almost fall into the hands of the Arsenal players as they thrilled fans with what Bastin would later describe as " … the best football I have ever seen".

Arsenal came out with all guns blazing for the 1930-31 season, losing just one game out of their first 18. During that run, there were four, 4-1 victories, against Blackpool, Bolton Wanderers, Sunderland and Leicester City; on three occasions the Gunners hit home 5 goals, against Aston Villa, Middlesborough and Chelsea. As if that wasn't enough, the season got even better. Grimsby disappeared beneath a 9-1 onslaught; Leicester went down 7-2, Derby County vanished 6-2, and Bolton got slapped

grabbed 57 goals, a terrific tally that brought Arsenal home second in the table, 5 points behind Chapman's old club, Huddersfield. It had been nothing less than a meteoric rise. The manager's new style, employing counter-attacking football, speedy wingers and a strong defence, had paid dividends.

Unfortunately, although this season hinted at what could be achieved, the Gunners' performances failed to match up to the high hopes with which everyone had started out in the new season. As it turned out, Chapman's five-year plan turned out to be spot on.

The next four seasons brought mediocre results that had fans thinking that the bad old days had returned. 11th, (despite a cracking season for James Brain, who whipped in 34 goals), 10th, 9th, and finally 14th. In 1930, Arsenal lost the last two games of that season. By then, Buchan

Sir John Norton Griffiths Arsenal Director 1928-1930

again even worse at the end of the season, 5-0. In the League, Arsenal had become unstoppable.

Three men did the greatest damage to the opposition; outside-left Cliff Bastin hit the net 29 times; David Jack scored 33; but it was Jack Lambert who hit the heights with a mighty 39 goals, to become top goalscorer in an incredible season of 127 goals in total. With 66 points, (a record not broken until 1969), and 7 points clear of Aston Villa, the Gunners lost just 5 matches, to become League Champions for the first time. Chapman had delivered on his promise, and for him and Norris, a dream had come true with a team that is still considered to be one of the best ever fielded at Arsenal. Four men in that team are in the top ten highest league goalscorers of all time at Arsenal; Bastin is third highest with 178 goals. Brain is sixth with 139, Hulme ninth on 125, and Jack is tenth with 124. It was a magical year.

1931-32 proved to be a hiccup in an unprecedented run of success for Arsenal. It wasn't a bad year at all; second place in the league just two points behind the champions is hardly a disaster even if it is disappointing to be so close and yet so far. The same can be said of the FA Cup final when Arsenal lost out to old rivals Newcastle United, 2-1, when a Newcastle goal was scored after the ball had apparently gone out of play. And there was a Charity Shield win against West Bromwich Albion, as a consolation prize. Yet the feeling was, of course, that the team had missed a beat after the immense promise of the year before. Lambert Hulme, Bastin and Jack were still banging in the goals regularly; Lambert's 26 made him top goalscorer, so no problems there. The defence was looking strong, and the addition of young goalkeeper Frank Moss in November 1913, and right-back George Male, who was to pair up with Hapgood because captain Tom Parker was winding down his career, made sure it stayed that way. Parker eventually left the club to manage Norwich, playing his last game for Arsenal in October 1932. So spirits were justifiably buoyant as the 1931-32 season got under way; the competition proved that the previous season had, indeed, been no more

London Derby at Highbury against Spurs October 20th 1934

round, by lowly Walsall. Faced with a trio of injuries and unfit star players, Chapman had opted for playing many of his reserves. In the mud of the field that day, the 14th January 1933, Walsall tackled hard and disrupted the makeshift Arsenal team. Black was at fault in both goals that went in against the Gunners as they went down 2-0 in what was described as the most stunning act of giant-killing in the history of the FA Cup. Chapman was fuming, and Black's punishment was swift; he was banned from the Highbury ground and sold to Plymouth just days later.

It took Arsenal all of August and September of 1933 to find their rhythm, by which time their unnerved fans were beginning to wonder if the team was up to its old tricks. There was a 1-1 draw against Birmingham in the first match of the season, followed by two wins, two losses and two more draws; but suddenly, on September 30th at home to Middlesborough, the tide suddenly turned. Arsenal ramped up their challenge with just one loss in 16 games. They were top of the table in December, four points ahead with the title clearly in their sights.

Chapman must surely have been delighted at his team's performance. He caught a cold that winter, but he still travelled north to see Arsenal's upcoming opponents, Sheffield Wednesday, play. On his return south, he went to see the Arsenal third team play. The cold turned into severe pneumonia. On the 6th January 1934, Chapman died. The shock at Arsenal was indescribable; *"Herbert Chapman had been loved by us all"*, said Cliff Bastin. One of the greatest innovators and lovers of the game, the man who had skillfully created one of the greatest teams of the era, had been cruelly taken from them. He was just 55 years of age.

Chapman's death affected the players badly on and off the field. Arsenal lost 3 of their next 4 matches.

Arsenal director George Allison became acting manager, leaving the practical side to trainer Tom Whittacker and Joe Shaw in an attempt to minimise the disruption. Despite misgivings amongst some of the players, the decision proved to be spot on. Arsenal lost just two more games that season, to Leicester 4-1 and Portsmouth 1-0, and did honour to Chapman's memory by chalking up another 11 wins, finally beating Huddersfield Town to the league title by three points. Chapman had tightened up his defence to the point where, although the goals were less

than a hiccup … although there was to be a mighty sneeze before the season ended.

The Gunners were firing on all cylinders from the outset, and only two games got away from them in the course of nineteen played until the middle of December. The new west stand was opened on the 10th December, and from their new vantage point, the fans could watch the team deliver the wonderful, entertaining football that Chapman wanted from them. There were some magnificent victories; a 6-1 win against Sunderland, a 7-1 win against Wolverhampton wanderers, an 8-2 defeat of Leicester City and a 9-2 drubbing of Sheffield United. Bastin whacked home 33 goals in 43 outings, and only Ernest Coleman came close with 24. Oddly, four of Arsenal's nine defeats were at home. But those setbacks could not prevent the Gunners from streaming home at the end of the season, 4 points clear of Aston villa. A winning Arsenal line up would claim top place for the following two seasons as well.

The sneeze came in 1933 in the form of humiliation in the FA Cup third

Arsenal play Racing Club de France 1934

evident that season, Bastin was top goalscorer with just 15, the Arsenal back line was one of the hardest in the league to penetrate. One new signing Allison made in March, Ted Drake, proved his worth, too, with 7 goals in just 10 games.

After the success of a second league title in a row, Allison secured the manager's seat. It seemed a logical move. He knew that Chapman had considered that the team was aging and needed renewal, so Lambert, Jack and other older players were replaced, with Wilf Copping and Jack Crayston arriving to give vigour to the left-half and right-half spots. Allison's instincts matched those of his predecessor and Arsenal set out on what was to be a record-breaking season.

Yet with only 4 wins from 9 games at the start of 1934-35, it looked as though any glory that season might be hard to come by, despite Liverpool vanishing beneath an 8-1 onslaught by the Gunners in the second match of the season. Two runs of 4 victories in a row, one in January and one in April, not only spared the Gunners' blushes, but also took them to the top of the table and a third successive title, with 58 points, four points ahead of Sunderland. A momentous achievement.

Although the FA Cup dream faded, after a 2-1 loss to Sheffield Wednesday in round 6, the Charity Shield went to Arsenal with a 4-0 win against Manchester City. Ted Drake had proved to be an inspired choice, who even left the marvellous Cliff Bastin trailing in his wake as he roared on to a total of 42 goals in 41 league matches, an outstanding performance. There had been three hat-tricks and he had scored four goals on four separate occasions. He sailed on to become top goalscorer for 5 seasons, only being interrupted by the Second World War. His contribution to Arsenal's success had been immeasurable; and yet his hour of greatest glory was still to come.

A 3-1 win against Sunderland in the first match of 1935-36 seemed to auger well for the future. In one sense that was true. Silverware came to Arsenal that season, too, but if fans could have foreseen that 15 draws would be spattered throughout that year's games, then they might have predicted the inevitable final league result. There were exciting games and good score lines; 4-0 against both Wolverhampton and Derby, 5-1 against Blackburn.

And then there was that most incredible day that would be spoken of from father to son at Arsenal for generations.

It was the 14th December 1935. Arsenal were at villa Park to meet Aston Villa in front of 70,000 people. They were lucky enough to witness a display of football that remains unmatched in the top-flight English game. Because of injuries, neither James nor Hulme were on the field, but Drake, his knee bandaged, soared to the occasion. Despite Arsenal playing vigorous football it was Villa who dominated, but Drake was unstoppable. By half time he had scored a hat-trick to put the Gunners 3-0 ahead. In the second half he repeated his trick with another three goals and then added a 7th, so that Arsenal left the field 7-1 winners. Drake (together with James Ross of Preston) continues to hold the record for most goals scored in an elite-level league game, to this day.

The Daily Express rhapsodised over his performance:

"He is absolutely fearless, and up to Saturday his game generally had been a reflection of his immense physique. On Saturday he was transformed into a centre forward of the highest class. He … was brilliant in every phase of the game. He had six shots at goal in the first hour of the game. Every shot scored".

Sadly, the game was not one along the route to the league title. All the draws had sunk the Gunners to 6th at the close of the season. But Drake's personal glory was not over and neither was Arsenal's.

With a 5-1 win against Bristol Rovers under their belt in round three of the FA Cup run, they hummed along smoothly to the final against Sheffield United. Allison knew he had to field a strong team for the final and so he spared his best players in the last league games; the club was hit by a £250 fine as a result. United started strongly, but neither side could strike home for most of the nail-biting game. Drake, recovering from a cartilage operation, had put away 27 goals that season, but the most important strike was the one he made that 25th of April 1936, 15 minutes from time. Thanks to his goal, Arsenal lifted the trophy for the second time. The team had now won four league championships and two FA Cups in seven years, a wonderful testament to the man who had started the golden years; Herbert Chapman.

Such were the wonderful successes buzzing in everyone's memories, when the 1936-37 turned out to be a wet squib. Perhaps the aging team that Allison had nurtured was losing its sting, but having slipped to 17th by the autumn, the decline was serious and had to be stopped. And stopped it was as Arsenal shot back up the table to top position. Just two games

FA Cup Final Arsenal V Sheffield United 25th April 1936

lost in 26 outings meant the Gunners were a side to fear once more. Sadly the top spot was only held temporarily, and losing 2-0 away twice, to Manchester City — who won the championship — and Chelsea, left them in third place at the end of the 1937 competition. FA Cup dreams that year had floated away with a 3-1 defeat to West Bromwich Albion.

Arsenal lost one of their superstars when Alex James retired on May 1st 1937. The unkempt inside-left has been described as a football genius. His contribution to the Arsenal success story is immeasurable and he remains one of the footballing giants.

It was with some trepidation that fans waited on the terraces for the first match of the new season. Changes to the team earlier in the year had not produced the desired trophy-winning combination. Yet despite a dip in Drake's goal-scoring tally to 18 — Kirchen also fell back from 22 to 8, and Davidson from 11 to 2 — Bastin more than doubled his previous season's total to net 17. There were 11 losses in 1937-38, whereas there had been just 8 in 1936-37. There were some wonderful matches to savour; 5-0 against Wolverhampton Wanderers in the third game of the season; 4-1 against Leeds United; 5-1 against Grimsby Town and 5-0 against Bolton Wanderers at the end of the season. Everything hinged on that final match because if fellow contenders Wolverhampton Wanderers won their last match, they would become league champions. They lost. Arsenal had done just enough to finish top of the table, one point clear, even though they had won one game less than the previous season. They were champions for the fifth time.

No one could know it, but for Arsenal this was to be the last championship success for ten years. By the end of the season, Europe was rigid with tension because Hitler had annexed Austria and Czechoslovakia in March. The Gunners' form began to waver as events in Europe became ever more threatening.

In the 1938-39 season, only Ted Drake maintained his impressive form. 14 goals came from his boot, whilst Kirchen could only manage 9 and Bastin hit just 4, in 24 matches. There were only 7 wins to cheer about until the end of the year and an equal number of losses. Although more victories cheered the fans the following year, 1939, another 7 defeats prevented a serious league challenge. Arsenal came home fifth, 12 points behind the leaders Everton. There had been no glorious 5-goal feasts; fans used to goal bonanzas had to be content with a 4-1 defeat of

FA Cup Final Alex James with the Cup after defeating Sheffield United 25th April 1936

Stoke City. The FA Cup was over in round 6 against Chelsea with a 1-0 defeat. Winning the Charity Shield was the consolation prize; 2-1 against Preston North End.

Uncertainty hung over everyone in Britain in September 1939. The league fixtures began nonetheless, only to be stopped after three matches. Arsenal were third having lost one and won two games. Then war against Germany was declared. The killing was to start all over again.

The 65th season of competitive league football in England was abandoned in September 1939. Instead, regional league competitions were set up, although over half of the teams then resigned because they could not fulfill all of their fixtures.

Once again, Arsenal players and supporters changed into battle gear. There were forty-four professional players at Highbury at the beginning of the war. Forty-two of those entered the armed forces. Nine never came back home. They were among many other footballers who gave their lives to fight dictatorship. Because of their sacrifice, and the courage of countless others, football was able to continue in freedom after the war.

Here are the names of the Arsenal players who died;
Henry Cook • Bobby Daniel • William Dean • Hugh Glass • Leslie Lack •
William Parr • Sidney Pugh • Herbie Roberts • Cyril Tooze

No other club suffered so many deaths amongst players as Arsenal did.

Whilst most men went into the army, Drake, Hapgood, Crayston and Kirchen, amongst others, joined the RAF. Trainer-physiotherapist Tom Whittaker was a squadron leader and eventually awarded an MBE for his actions.

Highbury became an ARP (Air Raid Precautions) base during the war, and because it was close to Kings Cross station, it was hit by bombs on several occasions, the worst being when a 1,000lb bomb came down in the practice field beside the stadium. On the 16th of April 1942, the Luftwaffe dropped 100,000 incendiary bombs on London....

....Highbury received its share and five incendiary bombs set fire to the roof of the North Bank and the Laundry End, causing it to collapse.

THE POST WAR YEARS

When the fighting was over, only the FA Cup competition was resumed for the 1945/46 season. The FA introduced home and away legs that year, so that the clubs could earn money while the league was not operating. The league started up again in 1946/47, and all teams resumed playing in the same division that they were in when games were suspended in 1940.

It was a very different Arsenal team that ran out onto the field on August the 31st 1946 than the one that had competed before the war.

There was no Hapgood, no Copping, no Kirchen, no Jack Crayston and no Drake. Drake had suffered a slipped disc so his playing career had come to end. George Male, Reg Lewis and Cliff Bastin were back as were the two Comptons, Dennis and Les. But it soon became clear that there was a lot of work to be done if the Gunners were to regain the form that had brought so much glorious success between the wars.

The start of the season was horrible; 3 losses in 4 games, which included a 6-1 whack around the head from Wolverhampton Wanderers in the first league game of 1946. Two wins were followed by another three losses, one of which was a 5-2 defeat to Manchester United. And so it went on, with Arsenal a very uncomfortable second from bottom in December.

Fortunately, by the middle of December, Allison was able to buoy up the sinking ship. He had made two great acquisitions, players that were, in fact, past their best; Walley Barnes was 35 and Ronnie Rooke was 32. But Allison was looking for experience rather than brilliance; he needed men who could anchor the team and at least save it from destruction. His plan worked, and the team began to bring home more victories than defeats. There were even hints of the past, with a 4-1 defeat of Sunderland and a magnificent 6-2 walloping of Manchester United, plus an exciting game that produced a 5-3 win against Grimsby Town at Highbury. The last game of the season was given away to Sheffield United, 2-1 but the Gunners were safe by then although far from glory, on 13th place. Reg Lewis proved that he had lost none of his verve, hammering home 29 goals, with Ronnie Rooke not far behind on 22, so Allison's £1,000 for the player had been well spent.

Allison had concentrated on saving the Gunners from relegation, but everyone could sense that an era had come to end. The great runs of trophies and titles of the pre-WWII years would not be seen again until the 1980s. Changes were coming to Highbury. The first of these was Allison's departure; he was in his mid-sixties and some forty years of association with the Gunners came to an end. Cliff Bastin had been hampered by injury and increasing deafness and also retired from the game that season.

Arsenal captain George Male leads out the team at Highbury. 17th August 1946

Tom Whittaker had been quietly training the Arsenal players and was also the team physiotherapist, winning the trust of the players and gaining the nickname 'Magic Hands' in the process. The players wanted the board to appoint Whittaker as the new manager. Shy of publicity and preferring his backroom job, Whittaker eventually succumbed and accepted the position of secretary-manager. Continuity had been maintained.

Whittaker certainly proved his worth, staying with the team until 1956 and chauffeuring it through its final period of glory before the drought set in for seventeen long years.

Whittaker's revamped team held new players Archie Macauley from Brentford and Don Roper from Southampton. Roper didn't let the team down, hitting in 10 goals that season from his position as winger.

It was a dream start for the Gunners. 17 games without a defeat sent them top of the table; they romped to 6 straight victories in the first 6 games. The fans were already sensing a season to remember when the team scythed through Charlton Athletic in a terrific 6-goal festival, winning 6-0 in front of the home crowd. Sunderland and Manchester United also felt the lash of the Gunner's whip.

But the glorious start had taken its toll and Rooke and Lewis, of all people, two centre forwards, were two of the men who fell prey to injuries. Whittaker had little money to buy talent to keep the momentum going; yet the first stumble only came at the end of November to Derby, and a 1-0 loss away from home.

Within two days in December, Liverpool were beaten 3-1 and then beat Arsenal 2-1; this defeat heralded another 6-match run of victories. There were to be just four more defeats that season as the Gunners fought their way to the top. New signing, wing-half Alex Forbes, ran onto the field for

Chelsea v Arsenal Rooke of Arsenal leaps for the ball 20th January 1947

his debut against Wolverhampton Wanderers and had two goals to his credit in his 11 appearances that season. Lewis and Roper hit 14 and 10 goals apiece whilst Rooke tore through the opposition defences to net 33. This trio put paid to Wolverhampton, 5-2, Middlesborough, 7-0 and in a mighty flourish in the last game of the season, sent fans into delirium in an 8-goal feast against Grimsby. Arsenal were crowned with the league championship for the sixth time, 7 points ahead of Manchester United, who they had beaten at home and taken a draw from at Old Trafford that season. A happy club could forget the FA Cup humiliation at the hands of Bradford Park from the second division, 1-0 in the third round.

For another Arsenal stalwart, George Male, it was the end of his career. The man who had set a record by being the first player in league

history to appear in six title-winning seasons, became an Arsenal trainer having been captain, and made 318 outings for the Gunners. This truly marked the end of an era, the final connection with the great days of Herbert Chapman.

In contrast to the excitement earlier in the year, the new season got off to a mediocre start with just one win in the first six games, 3-0 against Stoke City. Two 5-0 victories were highlights in what was otherwise an uneventful season that brought in a disappointing 5th place. Doug Lishman had arrived to bolster the team at inside-forward from where he hit home 13 goals, but Whittaker was unable to lift the team that had excited the fans the previous season, to new glory. The Charity Shield was the only award that came their way, wrested, satisfyingly, from

Arsenal v Burnley Burnley goalkeeper goes up to punch clear during the match at Highbury 16th December 1950

Manchester United, 4-3. But fans must have wondered where the Arsenal train was heading after star player Ronnie Rook left Highbury at the season's end. He was 37.

The fears seemed to be justified when Arsenal lost the first five games of the 1949-50 season. Then it seemed that great things might be possible after all; a run of 12 games without defeat began in September with a 2-1 win against West Bromwich Albion. That hope dribbled away with indifferent form for the rest of the season which left the team on 6th place. The fans were sent home with a blazing 5-2 performance against Stoke City, a score last seen against Everton in October of the previous year.

Perhaps the elation of a match that took place on April the 29th had given the team wings again.

Arsenal had run out onto the turf at Wembley to face Liverpool in the FA Cup final.

Arsenal win the 1950 FA cup final against Liverpool. Joe Mercer holds the cup aloft

This match was to be Joe Mercer's cup final, the day he had been dreaming of for as long as he could remember. He had just been voted Football Writer's Footballer of the Year, and was a very popular Arsenal player. Now he wanted an FA Cup winner's medal.

Whittaker almost decided against putting Roger Lewis on the field, worried about his ability to maintain the concentration that would be needed to beat a team of Liverpool's calibre. Mercer was captain and insisted on Lewis being included. Lewis then repaid the confidence in grand style with the two goals in the 17th and 63rd minutes that gave Arsenal Cup glory once again.

Again, the momentum could not be sustained and two indifferent years followed.

Yet the 1950-51 season started in great style with just two losses from nineteen games. New players were coming in and there was a 6-2 drubbing of Huddersfield Town, and two 5-1 victories, against Sunderland and Fulham, to get fans cheering. All seemed to be going well. And then, with a loss to Bolton Wanderers, 3-0, in December, the Arsenal train was derailed. Injuries to Lishman (who still became top goalscorer with 17) and keeper George Swindin didn't help, as Arsenal drifted and finally landed on 5th place. By that time, the FA Cup had become a battle for another year after a 5th round loss to Manchester United, 1-0.

In 1951-52 there were improvements that brightened the atmosphere at Highbury. And these were not just due to the new floodlighting that was switched on that season. With three losses in 17 games, the Gunners were contending for the top places and there was hope again. Some even dared to hope for the double; until a spell of 3 defeats in 4 matches, starting with a 2-0 defeat to Newcastle United in November, rather dampened the joy, briefly. But Arsenal put themselves back in contention, losing just one game out of the next fifteen.

Luck was not on Arsenal's side, however, and injuries began to affect results. Both Ray Daniel and Lionel Smith went down, and Mercer, no longer the youngest player on the field, was showing signs of tiredness. Yet although all was lost in theory, the last game of season against Manchester United might have produced a miracle and the league title.

Arsenal v. Fulham Arsenal centre-forward Holton takes on goalkeeper Flack 27th October 1951

FA Cup semi-final Arsenal v Chelsea Arsenal goalkeeper, Swindin saves a Chelsea header 7th April 1952

Manchester's six goals put paid to that bubble in a 6-1 defeat at Old Trafford. Close, and yet so far.

Arsenal had reached the FA Cup final in 1952. Yet with so many injuries, Arthur Shaw, for example, was missing having broken his wrist, the struggle proved too much for the Gunners, who went down 1-0. So ended a season of frustration and near misses.

Frustration that was followed by a seventh league title won after a nail-biting race to the top. Not that anyone could have imagined that scenario as the season got under way. Six wins in fourteen games was not a record designed to inspire confidence; especially as it included two home

defeats to Sunderland, 1-2, and Carlton Athletic, 3-4. From November results began to improve but not enough to make any game certain. The Gunners were capable of thrashing Liverpool in an astonishing 5-1 victory at Anfield and then losing at home to Cardiff 1-0. They might hammer in 6 against Derby County and then draw with West Bromwich Albion 2-2 at Highbury. Losing a point to Preston at home in a 1-1 draw almost cost them the title as the season shrank. But luck was on their side, and with five games won in succession, including a 4-2 away victory against Manchester City, and seven games without defeat, Arsenal were fighting for the top spot. Every Arsenal fan must have thought that they

34

Arsenal v Blackpool Cliff Holton, Arsenal centre-forward shoots for goal 28th December 1953

would not be able to stand the strain when the Gunners went to Deepdale to play rivals Preston North End in the penultimate game. Both clubs were on equal points at that stage; Arsenal had a game in hand and a superior goal difference, so a win would have helped everyone's blood pressure. Preston won 2-0 with help from the wonderful Tom Finney. All now depended on the last game against Burnley; at home.

On the 1st May, 51,500 people crammed into Highbury. Spirits were high before the worst nightmare a player can suffer, became reality; Mercer deflected a Burnley cross into his own goal. The Arsenal supporters' hearts were in their mouths. Despite the setback, the Gunners defence worked solidly to allow 'the Arsenal three', Lishman, Logie and Forbes, to work their magic. Each of them hit the Burnley net before half-time. Relief on the Arsenal terraces was palpable. The second half was one to savour; Burnley fought like tigers to get back into the game and managed to pull one back making the excitement almost unbearable, until the final whistle sent the Arsenal fans wild. For the seventh time, with a 3-2 win, Arsenal were league champions, by a goal difference of 0.099.

What happened after that? What indeed. Many people have tried to find the answer to that question. The facts are plain enough; Arsenal suffered a ghastly, sixteen-year famine with no major silverware to show for their efforts. It was a dire period in the club's history.

The best that can be said of the Gunners see-sawing form is that at least they did not have to cope with the humiliation of relegation. In fact, during all those years of dashed hopes, 14th was the lowest position they occupied, with a 3rd position in 1959 giving a pale echo of past glory.

That period of famine was ushered in with the passing of a Highbury star; Alex James. His death from cancer in London on June 1st 1953, shocked everyone; he was just 51 years old, and in retrospect his death seemed to portend the struggles that the team would experience over the forthcoming years.

When the 1953-54 season got under way, the Gunners ran into trouble immediately, chalking up just one victory in the first ten games. They lost two games at Highbury, drew three and then crashed 7-1 at Sunderland. Fans were already beginning to fear the worst before manager Whittaker was able to stem the rot with a 2-0 defeat of Chelsea, revenge for a 2-1 loss against the Pensioners at Highbury the previous week.

Arsenal V Spartak Moscow 9th November 1954

For a brief period, the gods were with the team, and a run of ten games brought just one defeat against Burnley. But even then, losing 5-2 at in front of the home crowd was not exactly designed to inspire anyone.

Whittaker brought in Tommy Lawton. It was a gamble that did not pay off, for the aging star player, he was 34 years old when he arrived at Highbury, could not recapture his former glory days. He went on to score fifteen goals over two seasons, although the fans had to wait many months for the first of those. Lawton was never certain of a place in the first eleven.

A mediocre season that had seen Arsenal hit the bottom of the league table at one stage, limped home; not, however, before Joe Mercer had suffered a double fracture of his leg in a 3-0 win against Liverpool. His misfortune was in tune with Arsenal's; he was stretchered from the field. His 275-match Arsenal career was over. Mercer had been an inspirational captain who had led the team out to some of the great victories of the late nineteen-forties and early fifties. Mercer retired, became a journalist and ran his grocer's shop in Wallasey on Merseyside before returning to the game as manager of Sheffield United in 1955.

A 3-1 win against Middlesborough finished an Arsenal season which left them stranded on 12th place in the table. As so often, the Charity

Shield in October 1953, won in a 3-1 victory against Blackpool, was the only compensation for a season that had least ended without disaster.

The best the Gunners could manage for the next three seasons was fifth. They hit that position twice in a row in 1955-56 and 1956-57 having bounced up from 9th in 1954-55 when even a wonderful ten-game winning streak could not wipe out the defeats of an indifferent start. Fortunately, Doug Lishman was ever watchful up front and could be relied on to get a decent quota of goals each year; which was just as well, or history might be telling a different story.

The onset of this unsettling period was made worse when the news came in that Tom Whittaker had died. The man who had taken over from an Arsenal giant, Herbert Chapman, and had steered the club towards the heights since 1947, had worn himself out with the strain of running a major club. Whittaker died of a heart attack, in University College Hospital, London, at the age of 58. It was truly the end of an era, for Whittaker was the last of the secretary managers at Arsenal.

The board decided to promote Bob Wall to secretary, whilst Jack Crayston became permanent manager in December 1956. Crayston's period of tenure was brief, only lasting until May 1958, and it frustrated and disappointed both him and the fans. With help from Ron Greenwood,

Chelsea v Arsenal Dodgin & Charlton of Arsenal battle Tindall of Chelsea 26th October 1957

who came to Arsenal in the winter of 1957 and was widely considered to be one of the most talented coaches in the country, Crayston managed to keep the team in 5th place in his first year, but 14 points separated them from Manchester United at the top. Crayston was unable to persuade the Arsenal board to invest in the new players he knew were vital if the team was to be rejuvenated with young blood. The
players were capable of success; 7-3 against Manchester City; 4-0 against Birmingham City; 6-3 against Sheffield Wednesday. Yet a 6-2 defeat to Manchester United, another, 5-2 against Wolverhampton Wanderers and then a 3-1 defeat against Luton Town told the other side of the story.

When the club finished 12th the following season, the worst placing for twelve years, the game was over for Crayston. The victories had been hard to come by, and Northampton Town of the Third Division South had humiliated the team in the FA Cup; Northampton won 3-1. Crayston felt that he could not do justice to the club without money to fund the squad and left to join Doncaster Rovers.

With change in the air, former Arsenal goalkeeper George Swindin was chosen as the new manager, working in tandem with Ron Greenwood and the pairing seemed to work wonders for the team.

A young man by the name of Tommy Docherty arrived at Arsenal to play at wing-half; Docherty later found fame as manager of Manchester United and the Scottish national team. He would stay at Arsenal until 1961.

Preston brought the club down to earth with a 2-1 defeat in the first game in autumn 1958, but a run of six games with one defeat, which included a 5-1 defeat of Leicester City and two 6-1 victories, first against Everton and then against Bolton Wanderers, had the fans sensing that this might be a season to cheer about. Despite centre-forward David Herd striking home 18 times, those goal scores could never be repeated, however, and two lean periods robbed the Gunners of any trophies. The season highlight was a 3-2 defeat of Manchester United. Three home defeats in four matches, against Blackpool, Aston Villa and Preston, and then another dip in form in February 1959 followed by seven games with not a single win, found the club on third position at the end of the season.

It turned out to be the best they could manage for another twelve years.

Money was still a problem. Without the players to win games, the crowds shrank, and so the gate receipts shrank, too; a vicious circle that found Arsenal under Swindin's leadership enter the new decade of the swinging sixties, ambling home in 13th, 11th and 10th positions, and never get further than round three in the FA Cup. Top-flight players such as Danny Clapton and George Eastham were unable to stop the gangrene that had set in; neither was centre-forward David Herd, who had his best season ever in 1960-61 when he whacked home 30 goals in what proved to be his last season for the Gunners.

By 1961-62 it was blindingly clear that Swindin was not going to be able to turn the tide. In the search for a replacement, the board did something they had never done before; they appointed a man who had no connections with the club, a man who was a legend in British football.

Billy Wright had captained England a record 90 times, had been the first player to step out 100 times for the English national team, and had played in 105 matches for the national squad. He had spent his entire career at Wolverhampton Wanderers, and had been the England youth squad manager since 1960 before joining Arsenal; it was his first major managerial post. A gamble for the Arsenal board; a gamble that did not pay off.

In this new, changed world of the nineteen-sixties, violence on the terraces and towns began to raise its ugly head. The mild-mannered Billy Wright was a voice from another, gentler age and although he knew talent when he saw it, he was unable to mould his team into a squad that could aggressively storm a path through the dangerous jungle that the Football League had now become.

Proof of his eye for talent came in the shape of centre-forward Joe Baker, who treated fans to 31 goals in his first season, 1962-63. Ian Ure, Frank McLintock, and another legend, goalkeeper Bob Wilson came to Arsenal, as did a future Gunner's star, Charlie George, who started out in his career under Wright's tutelage.

Yet the winning results against the important clubs would not come in. The season began well, two wins, two matches, which put Arsenal second in the division; but in a dreadful run of just two wins in thirteen games, starting with a home defeat to Manchester United 3-1, the die had been cast before the season was two months old, and Arsenal were 7th at the close of the season. That was the highest position that they had occupied since August the previous year.

Wright stayed at Arsenal until 1966. The league tables tell their own tale of woe; 8th, 13th, and 14th in Wright's last season; the last time they had hit that spot was in the 1929-30 season.

Thank God for Baker, the fans might have chanted as he chalked up another 31 goals in 1963-64 and then 25 the year after. In the year Wright walked away from Highbury for the last time, the centre-forward managed to net just 13. And with that he was the highest scorer at the club. It was indeed a sad time for the proud North Londoners.

The board took the only decision they could, and Wright was told of his dismissal when he arrived back from holiday. He had wanted to be the man to take the club back to the heights, and he left with a heavy heart.

"He had", said football writer Brian Glanville, *"neither the guile nor the authority to make things work, and he reacted almost childishly to criticism".*

His fault was to be a gentleman in an age when football was becoming ever more hard-nosed.

Arsenal goalkeeper, Jim Furnell snatches ball away from Chelsea's Barry Bridges 26th September 1964

THE BERTIE MEE ERA

W hoever took over at Arsenal in the mid-sixties was going to take over a potential nightmare. With the team's form declining there was only a short step to be taken before the manager would be presiding over a relegation side and the inevitable vitriol from all around.

In this atmosphere of gloom, the board once again made a brave decision. Looking to men within the club again, the chairman, Dennis Hill-Wood brought the club's physiotherapist into the limelight to fill the hot seat. His choice was inspired.

"If that is what the board would like ..." said the new manager and set out to turn the Gunner's fortunes around; his name was Bertie Mee.

Betram Mee had been working as a physiotherapist at Arsenal since 1960 and was known as a disciplinarian, a man who could spot talent, and an organisational genius. There were few at the time who thought that he would last the course; Mee proved them all wrong in blazing style. In coach Don Howe he had one of the best men at his side that he could wish for and when he also engaged Dave Sexton to work alongside Howe, he had assembled a winning combination. Mee, who admitted that his tactical knowledge left a lot to be desired, could safely leave the intricacies of match play in the firm hands of these two men. With Mee's measured approach complimenting Howe's more emotional but spot-on analyses, after 17 years, the climb back out of the pit of desperation could finally begin.

Albeit for a brief moment of brilliance.

New players brought in by Mee, men such as George Graham from Chelsea and Bob McNab from Huddersfield, did not have an immediate effect on the field although it might have seemed so after the great start to the 1966-67 season with three straight wins. That only happened three times that season, and those times were punctuated with just two wins in a 17-game run, and a ten-game run with just two wins and six draws. Graham was top goalscorer with a paltry 12 goals when Arsenal finished on 7th position. In 1967-68, however, his tally was 21 even though Arsenal

were in an even worse position; 9th. Finishing the season with a flourish, winning their last five games, the Gunners gave a tantalising sign of things to come. Arsenal had even gone through to the final of the League Cup, where they had lost 1-0 to Leeds United. One of the teams they beat in that last league dash was Leeds, so the 4-3 defeat of the northerners was, at least, a satisfying revenge.

No trophies then, as yet, but Mee was pulling his team out of the soft approach that he had inherited from Billy Wright and could see that his men were taking on a more steel-like attitude. They needed it, if they were to survive the new aggresive, increasingly efficient style of the professional game.

1968-69 was a test for fans because the team were still not quite good enough for the top. They were showing fighting spirit, however, and as the decade drew to a close they gave their fans a start to the season to be proud of, their nine games without defeat sending them into first place for several weeks. And there were some great matches to cheer the fans' hearts, including a 2-1 defeat of their great rivals Tottenham. There were decisive victories against Manchester United, 3-0, Manchester City, 4-1 and Sheffield Wednesday, 5-0. But the goals were not plentiful up front with only John Radford on 19 anywhere near the 20 mark. Also, the 15th of March 1969 will go down in club history as one of those humiliating cup ties that descended only too regularly upon the Gunners. Having overcome Tottenham in two games, third division Swindon Town were their opponents in the final. Swindon dominated the game. The newspapers ranted about Arsenal's *"shame"*. One report read: *"Arsenal, slaves of their own system, methodical but utterly predictable, were finally unhinged by the individual brilliance and flair of the Swindon stars – the small town Cinderellas whom cynics expected to lose to the North London favourites by a bucketful of goals"*.

The score; 3-1 to Swindon. Enough said about that.

Bob Wilson made a comment about what happened after that defeat to Swindon:

Bertie Mee chats to some of the players at Highbury 12th August 1966

"It's never going to remain the happiest day of my life, but I will go to the grave telling people that what we achieved in the years following that League Cup defeat we owe to Swindon. There were certain players who dropped by the wayside, but those who were part of the abuse we got from the London press — who thought there was no way we could lose to a Third Division side — used it as a spur".

Fans would have been hard pressed to have recognised any *"spur"* in 1969-70; that ignominious defeat, it seemed, carried its poison over into the next season. John Radford showed consistency with another 19 goals. Charlie George had made the first team and the Highbury star was in the ascendent. Nonetheless, the Gunners never rose higher than 7th and languished around the middle of the table for most of the league competition with 18 matches drawn and 12 won, and they lost twice to both their London rivals Tottenham and Chelsea; not a happy resumé. They did manage to beat West Ham; once, at home 2-1; but by then, the League title (Arsenal were 12th), the League Cup and the FA Cup had flapped off elsewhere.

1968 League Cup Final, Leeds v Arsenal, trouble breaks out 2nd March 1968

And by then a miracle had occurred.

The Inter-Cities Fairs Cup had started in 1955, and Arsenal had qualified by grabbing fourth place in the league in 1969. In contrast to their performances in other competitions they had given their fans joy by powering through the knockout rounds in the Fairs Cup. Among others, Sporting Lisbon fell before the Gunners in a thrilling 3-0 return leg at Highbury, and Dinamo Bicau from Romania were crushed 7-1, also at Highbury. Arsenal survived a wobble when they lost 1-0 to Ajax but went through on a 3-1 aggregate only to lose to Anderlecht away, in the first leg of the final, again 3-1. This left them with an uphill struggle of huge proportions. Especially considering their league form. Although disheartened after the defeat,

Captain Frank McLintock refused to bow down, and his fighting spirit fired the rest of the team; the results may have been poor that season, but the captain had proven that he was a man to be reckoned with. The Scottish national team had already recognised his worth. And when the 28th of April 1970 arrived, Arsenal were ready to take on the world.

Twenty-five minutes passed before the Anderlecht spell was broken. Midfielder Eddie Kelly, Mee's 'midfield tank', scored three goals that season, and none more important than the one he fired in against Anderlecht that day. Arsenal became unbeatable. Coming out for the second half, Radford had his chance in the 75th minute and Arsenal were two up. Anderlecht attacked and opened up the field leaving another midfielder, John Sammels, space to put in the third. The drought was over for fans

Arsenal first team squad 1969

European Fairs Cup Semi-Final 1st Leg. Arsenal V Ajax. Arsenal's Eddie Kelly heads the ball away during an Ajax attack 8th April 1970

and players; Bertie Mee's men were European champions and Arsenal had their first trophy for 17 years. It was, as can be imagined, a night of ecstatic rejoicing.

How often have the supporters hoped that the successes of one season can be carried through to the next only to have those hopes dashed. Arsenal fans knew that feeling only too well. In 1970-71 that would not be their fate. They were destined to roar themselves hoarse.

Mee had built his team, and the names he had acquired are held high in the esteem of those aware of Arsenal's history; Charlie George; George Armstrong; John Radford; Bob Wilson; Frank McLintock; Eddie Kelly. Still, when the Gunners ran out to play against Everton on the 15th August 1970, Mee had no idea that this was to be their, and his, year of glory.

A 2-2 draw away from home against league champions Everton was satisfying, and so was the 0-0 draw away against West Ham, but no real indication of things to come. The 4-0 home win against Manchester United was much more exciting, before the first loss, to Chelsea, 2-1, kicked in. That put the team on 7th place.

By the time two memorable matches had taken place in September the Gunners were back on 3rd spot; they walloped West Bromwich Albion 6-2 away from home, were smacked in the head by Stoke City 5-0, despite having one of the toughest defensive line ups in the league, and then suddenly took off. Whatever Bertie Mee said to them, it did the trick, and the Gunners set off for the top, making the number two spot their own for most of the season.

Fellow title contenders Leeds, Tottenham, Wolverhampton and Liverpool all felt the sting in Arsenal's game. The Highbury men racked up fourteen games without defeat, wobbled with two away defeats and then went on to thirteen matches with just one defeat. Excitement was building on the terraces and in the boardroom even though the League Cup had been thrown away with a loss to Crystal Palace, who eventually finished 18th in the table.

The Arsenal front guns were firing well, too; Charlie George claimed 10 goals that season and became an Arsenal hero at the same time, not least because he scored twice in the FA Cup against Manchester City to put the Gunners through to the quarter final; George Graham was on 14, Ray Kennedy 26 and John Radford 21. That inexplicable

George Armstrong in action

Charlie George takes on Willie Carlin of Leicester City

Bob Wilson keeps alert 25th March 1972

defeat to Stoke could well have put paid to their league title hopes, though, and it certainly made for a photo finish in May 1971, especially when the Gunners fell 1-0 to their nearest rivals, Leeds United, in April.

Another trophy, the Inter-Cities Fairs Cup, had slipped from the holders' grasp at Cologne in a 2-2 quarter final draw over two legs which gave Cologne the away goal advantage. That was on the 23rd March. On the 27th, Stoke were the opposition in the FA Cup and nearly sank the Gunners again, leading 2-0 at half time. The legendary Gordon Banks was beaten twice in the second half to spare the Arsenal blushes. On the 31st, Stoke were at the wrong end of the Gunner's wrath in the FA Cup semi-final replay going down 2-0 with Kennedy and Graham getting the honours.

Now there was the tantalising prospect of the double to electrify the Highbury crowd. It all hinged on the last games. After the defeat against Leeds, Arsenal had two games to play, Leeds had one, which they won. Arsenal were second in the table.

On the 1st of May, Stoke were back at Highbury; it was as though the gods were willing to give Arsenal the chance to truly wipe out the memory of that absurd defeat. Eddie Kelly made sure that Banks could not get in the way of Arsenal's march to the top, and Arsenal emerged the winners, 1-0.

That left Tottenham, who were in front of their home crowd for the match that could make or break Arsenal, on the 8th of May. A 0-0 draw would suffice for the title to go to the Gunners. The rivalry was intense between the two London clubs, and 50,000 crowded into the stadium at White Hart Lane.

The Gunners took their fans to the edge. With three minutes to go the match was goalless, until Ray Kennedy rose up to a George Armstrong cross, and the Arsenal supporters went wild as the ball went in past Pat Jennings. A three-minute onslaught by Tottenham could not prevent their London neighbours from basking in glory as the final whistle released them all from their agony. Arsenal were top of the table and League champions again for the first time since 1953. What better preparation for the FA Cup final one week later?

Arsenal ran out on the Wembley turf on the 8th May still elated from their title win. They were facing a formidable opponent; Bill Shankley's Liverpool. For 90 minutes the teams cancelled each other out. Then, in extra time, the game burst into life. Liverpool went ahead after two minutes with a Steve Heighway goal. Next, Eddie Kelly's equaliser was claimed by George Graham; ownership was not so important; the main thing was that Arsenal were still in the game. With the clock ticking, Radford sent an increasingly tired-looking Charlie George goal-wards once more. Striking the ball from 20 yards out, George's shot was a bullet that deflected off a defender and hit the Liverpool net. It was, as the saying goes, all over bar the shouting. And what shouting there was. Arsenal had emerged from years in the wilderness to pull off the league and cup double.

Sadly all fairy tales must all come to an end, and for Arsenal fans another dry period set in, not so long-lasting as the first, but at seven years it was a good biblical length for a famine. It was punctuated by one trophy before the club set off on another seven-year trip into the wilderness.

The year following the Double was indifferent; perhaps this was due to the fact that Don Howe had gone to manage West Bromwich Albion. Alan Ball arrived and took up his midfield position but could not prevent Arsenal from bouncing around between eighth and fourteenth to finally settle on fifth position. The League Cup and European Champions Cup, as it was now known, were lost, and the FA Cup final clash between Arsenal and Leeds went in the northerners favour, 1-0. Mee knew changes were needed but his decisions brought no better results. McLintock went to QPR, George Graham went to Manchester United.

Arsenal fared better the following year in what was to prove one of their best seasons, with a second place; they would not be placed higher again until 1989. Radford on 19 goals and Ball with 14 were an effective duo combining with George and Kennedy, but they could not lift the team to the top and the Gunners ended 3 points adrift of Liverpool. After that the team lost its bite and fell to 10th and then 16th in 1974-75. They were struggling to find form.

By 1976, Ray Kennedy and Charlie George had left the club and Mee himself, had exhausted his ambition. He had given the Club back its pride for a brief and glorious moment. Now he decided to retire.

It was former Northern Ireland international and Arsenal captain Terry Neill's time to take up the reigns and try to steer Arsenal's fortunes, which he did until 1983, when he, too,

realised that he was not going to be able to bring the Gunners back to lasting success.

A SUDDEN FLASH OF GLORY

Arsenal arrived at the mid-point of the famine in 1978 having lived through three more years of unsatisfying results; 7th, 8th and 5th places in the League. Always challenging, but just behind the big boys. Terry Neil made many changes to the team that he had inherited; Liam Brady and Pat Jennings were at Highbury, Alan Ball was not and nor were Eddie Kelly and John Radford.

The 1978-79 season was as average as those that had gone before

had been, and there was no sign that anything was going to be different with three wins from the first twelve matches. The team held its own after that shaky start and moved around either side of the 4th place for some time. They were doing well enough until February of 1979 when they beat QPR away 2-1; and then it unravelled. There were just three more wins for the rest of the season, which left them on 7th place, 20 points behind the leaders Liverpool, who had 68 points.

In the League Cup, the club had gone through another of its periodic humiliations, beaten 1-3 by Rotherham. In the FA Cup they had a marathon third round and played Sheffield Wednesday a record five times before going through to round four with a 2-0 win. Then they had to go into a replay with Southampton, which they won 2-0. So against expectations they moved through to the final and opponents Manchester United.

It was an exciting match for Arsenal, who took a two-goal lead and held it for most of the match. Then just about five minutes before full-time, United got one back and then another. The stadium was crackling with emotion as Arsenal's Graham Rix hurtled down the left wing and sent a cross floating across the United goal. Alan Sunderland connected with the ball. His shot fired into the Manchester net and gave Arsenal a 3-2 lead. The Gunners had secured the FA Cup once more.

And once more the fans had to swallow disappointment as hope for trophies retreated in the seasons that followed. There were seven more years of famine, with a little relief in 1987 at the Football League Cup Final and a 2-1 defeat of Liverpool. There was no comfort in 1980. There was a fourth place in the League and no progress the League or FA Cups to cheer about. In fact, losing to Swindon Town 3-4 in the League Cup 5th round was not good for morale at all. So all Arsenal eyes were on Europe as the club struggled its way through to the final against Valencia. Arsenal went away empty-handed having gone down on penalties.

The stalwart defender Pat Rice moved on to join Watford that year at the age of 31. He had been Arsenal captain and had played in five FA Cup finals, clocking up 528 appearances for the Gunners. Little did he know, but he had not seen the last of the Gunners.

Hillsborough

Pat Rice emerges from the Hillsborough tunnel

empty-handed. In 1989-90 that is what happened to Arsenal. Alan Smith was top goalscorer with 13. Impressive wins were followed by defeats, and the inconsistent form led to very short cup runs and a fourth place at the end of the season.

Graham had bought the Swedish player Anders Limpar and goalkeeper David Seaman, regarded as the best goalkeeper ever to wear the Arsenal shirt, in the summer. With this new talent, the Gunners set off on another season when they would challenge Liverpool for the league title.

Despite having two points deducted after a mass brawl during the game with Manchester United in October, which the Gunners won 1-0, Arsenal did indeed challenge, with a remarkable achievement. They lost

Arsenal v Liverpool. Charlie Nicholas celebrates scoring the 2nd goal in the League Cup final April 1987

just one game in the entire season, to Chelsea at Stamford Bridge on the 2nd of February 1991, 2-1. There were terrific performances, with Smith hitting 28 goals and Limpar proving a delight to watch and a great asset to the team. Arsenal beat Chelsea 4-1, and Southampton 4-0; Liverpool 3-0 and Sheffield United 4-1. They hit the top of the table in January 1991 and never lost their grip, taking out Crystal Palace 4-0 and Aston Villa 5-0.

Although their cup form was poor, the League games gave fans more than enough to shout about. They were three points clear when they met QPR in April, having been eight points behind Liverpool after the points deduction the previous year. In the final two games, Arsenal showed what they were made of by thumping Manchester United 3-1, revenge for the 6-2 mauling in the League Cup, and crushing Coventry City 6-1. Arsenal

had proven their calibre, and they came home as deserving winners in the League, with 83 points, leaving Liverpool trailing in their wake on 76.

Graham had reason to be more than happy with the team he had assembled. That confidence was misplaced, as the first match of the 1991-92 season showed, a disappointing 1-1 home draw against QPR. This was followed by two 3-1 losses against Everton and Aston Villa, which dropped the club onto twenty-first position.

In September, Graham signed a man who was to become an Arsenal superstar; Ian Wright. He gave great firepower up front, finishing the season with a very creditable twenty-six-goal tally in his thirty-three games.

For a while this seemed to have done the trick; Southampton went

Tony Adams, Steve Bould and David O'Leary celebrate as Arsenal win the league 6th May 1989

Ian Wright celebrates FA Cup semi final victory over Spurs 4th April 1993

Ian Wright scores the winner in FA Cup Final Replay against Sheffield Wednesday 20th May 1993

down 4-0 and Chelsea 3-2. But the latter victory heralded a period when there were just three wins until February of 1992. That put paid to any title hopes, and a 17-game undefeated run to the end of the season was not enough to get the Gunners, who were capable of thrashing third-placed Sheffield Wednesday 7-1, off fourth place. An inexplicable FA Cup loss, to Wrexham, a League Cup exit in the 3rd round thanks to Coventry, and defeat to Benfica in the European Cup ensured that this was another frustrating season. Even the Charity Shield against Tottenham in August 1991 had ended in a 0-0 draw. For George Graham it felt like the lowest point of his career.

Graham must have wondered if he had lost his touch when two defeats started the 1992-93 season. Norwich beat the Gunners 4-2 at home in the first match and Blackburn Rovers completed the double, 1-0. Nerves were calmed with a 2-0 victory over Liverpool and seven games without defeat, which saw Chelsea and Manchester City overcome and Arsenal rise to the top spot. But then it all went wrong and the team never recovered. Defeat followed defeat, and victories were so thin on the ground that tenth was all that they could manage after the final league match in what had now become the Premier League.

What a spectacular year it had been nonetheless!

Arsenal had pushed their way through the League Cup rounds, beating Millwall on penalties, dispensing with Derby County, and luckily avoiding humiliation by scraping home against Scarborough, 1-0. Now, Sheffield Wednesday was their adversary in the final.

When the Wednesday goal went in, Arsenal hearts missed a beat. They had to wait until the twentieth minute for an equaliser from Paul Merson before the glorious moment twenty minutes from time when defender Steve Morrow was in the right place to win Arsenal the trophy.

And the Gunners still had their sights on the FA Cup. They were in the final and their opponents were … Sheffield Wednesday.

Arsenal had knocked out Tottenham and Leeds en route to the final and were, of course, confident that they could pull off another victory against the northerners. It was not quite so easy the second time around, and the sides parted with a 1-1 draw.

Five days later they met again. Again Arsenal were being held to a draw after Ian Wright's goal in the thirty-third minute was matched by one from Wednesday, twenty minutes into the second half. The game entered the last minute of extra time, and in an all-out attempt to lift the coveted trophy even Arsenal defender Linghan went forward for a corner at the Wednesday end. It was a mighty gamble. And it was Linghan who put the ball into the Wednesday net. It was a wonderful end to what had been a season of surprises and triumphs in which Ian Wright's star shone brightly. His haul in 1992-93 was 30 goals, and he maintained his top goalscorer status for six consecutive seasons.

David O'Leary ended his Arsenal career with the FA Cup final. The man who had been called *"a very special player"* by Bertie Mee, had started out as an Arsenal apprentice in 1973 and was now moving on to Leeds United after 722 appearances in the red shirt. Sadly for him, O'Leary suffered an Achilles tendon injury at Leeds and retired in 1995 but later became a football manager.

That year was going to be a hard one to follow and even though Ian Wright bettered his tally from the previous season with 35 goals, a personal best, Arsenal nestled into fourth position in the League one more time as though it were home from home. It was an indifferent year that threw up seventeen drawn games. Even the last two were lost; 2-0 to both West Ham and Newcastle. There was no joy to be had from the FA Cup or the League Cup either. Not even the Charity Shield, lost to Manchester United on penalties. Unlikely as it seemed, however, there was still hope of silverware; in Europe.

Sandwiched between those two final league defeats came the European Cup Winners Cup final in Copenhagen. Arsenal had beaten Paris St. Germain to get there and on the 4th of May 1994 they ran onto the pitch to face Parma. Without Ian Wright … and David Seaman had broken a rib and was on painkillers. The odds were against them. And their tenacity was rewarded. Parma's forwards were razor sharp, but it was Alan Smith who struck with his left foot to volley the ball home for Arsenal. The Londoners' defence with the inimitable Tony Adams, held tight, and the Gunners took home the Cup. It was a night to revel in.

A night that had to last for four years.

1994-95 was a disaster almost from the start. The team was on

fifteenth place in September. By the 8th of February 1995, the FA Cup, League Cup and UEFA Super Cup challenges had petered out, and on the 21st, George Graham was sacked, the same day that the club claimed a rare victory; 1-0 against Nottingham Forest. The discovery that Graham had accepted a huge illegal payment, an *"unsolicted gift"*, as he described it later, of £425,000, was his downfall.

Arsenal were guided to the end of the season by Stewart Houston, Graham's assistant. They lost the final of the European Cup Winner's Cup to Real Zaragoza, 2-1 in May and then landed on twelfth place in the League after losing to Chelsea 2-1 in their final game. A sad time for everyone.

Not even the talents of Dennis Bergkamp and David Platt, who joined for the next season, could bring in the honours. Nor Bruce Rioch who took over the reigns from Houston. Rioch's time at Highbury was short-lived; he managed to get the club up to fifth place in the League, but many players were dogged with personal problems and injuries. Wright was unhappy and wanted to leave. Rioch left just before the 1996-97 season got under way, after a dispute with the board of directors. It was a difficult time for the club.

Help was at hand, though, in the shape of a Frenchman who would revamp the Arsenal style of play, bring back the sting and the honours to go with it and have a huge impact on the club and English football.

Arsène Wenger needed no persuasion to join Arsenal, and within half an hour of meeting the club representatives the deal had been signed.

A new, exciting era was about to dawn at Highbury.

Arsenal v Sampdoria. Arsenal scoring in the European Cup Winners' Cup Semi-Final First Leg 6th April 1995

'LE PROFESSEUR' ARRIVES AT HIGHBURY

Wenger arrived to take charge in September 1996, too late to turn the team around completely that season, and when it ended, the Gunners were in third place; it was unclear exactly what Mr. Wenger had up his sleeve until the 1997-98 season kicked off. It was an interesting season to say the least. Eight of the players were now over thirty years of age. Wenger had brought in Patrick Vieira, Emmanuel Petit and Marc Overmars amongst others, but did not want to cause too much disruption. A wise decision, because the team found themselves unbeaten and on top of the Premier League after the eighth game, a 4-0 win against fellow Londoners West Ham. Ian Wright had now beaten Cliff Bastin's goal-scoring record by claiming a hat-trick against Bolton Wanderers two weeks before, which gave him 179 goals.

Overmars, Bergkamp and Wright were sparkling, and

a 5-0 win against Barnsley suggested that Arsenal were going to be unstoppable. And that was when they stumbled, losing four of the eight games in November and December. There was no explanation and even Wenger was bewildered. Whatever caused the dip in form, it vanished as quickly as it had come, and Arsenal fought their way back up the table from their sixth position at the end of December to remain unbeaten for the next eighteen games. Along the way they had picked up a tremendous victory against their closest rivals for the title, Manchester United, at Old Trafford, 1-0 through an Overmars goal, a superb 5-0 win against Wimbledon, and gone top of the table.

The only shadow was that, in the meantime, Chelsea had denied them the chance at the League Cup, beating them 3-4 on aggregate in the semi-final.

With three games left, Arsenal were top of the Premier League; and they had struggled a little, it's true, needing a penalty shoot-out to beat Port Vale and then again against West Ham, but they were in the FA Cup final. The fans knew they were on the cusp of another double. If Wenger's men could make it, the supporters would clasp the Frenchman to their hearts; the first step was to get just one win in the last three games to claim the league title.

On the 3rd of May 1998, Arsenal dismantled the Everton side to roar to a 4-0 victory and claim the championship. The first goal was an Everton own goal. Overmars thrilled the crowd with quicksilver feet and two goals, and Adams added his own. The first step had been taken in style; an exhilarated but exhausted Arsenal side conceded the last two games to Liverpool and Aston Villa.

The next test was on its way.

Newcastle and Arsenal lined up at Wembley on the 16th of May. Even without Bergkamp Arsenal had the game under control against a less than passionate Newcastle team. Overmars and Anelka took the honours in a 2-0 win giving the Londoners another league and FA Cup double; their second.

Ian Wright had played his last game for the club in October the previous

Arsène Wenger celebrates with the Premier League Trophy 3rd May 1998

63

Arsène Wenger with new signings, Marc Overmars & Emmanuel Petit

64

Team & fans celebrate 1998 **FA Cup Final win**

65

Dennis Bergkamp in action against Dynamo Kiev 21st October 1998

67

Fredeik Ljungberg takes on Jaap Stam 1st August 1999

Thierry Henry celebrates 9th March 1999

year and it was time for him to move on. At almost thirty-five years of age, he had played 279 matches for the club and scored 185 goals. Now his talents were to be employed at rival London club West Ham United.

There was plenty to shout about as Arsenal continued to play the scintillating football that Wenger wanted; except that for the next three seasons that was never quite enough to win the main trophies. The team hit second place three times in a row and won the Charity Shield twice in a row; not exactly the results that Wenger was looking for.

A soft start to the 1998-99 season robbed them of the league title; four draws in a row, and the title went to Manchester United by one point. The next season they lost out to a rampant Manchester for a second time by a much more emphatic figure; 71 points to 93. Beating them 2-1 in the Charity Shield was mild compensation indeed.

Nicolas Anelka moved on that year, 1999, and an Arsenal legend arrived; Thierry Henry, who immediately took over the top goalscorer hat and kept it for seven consecutive years. He went on to score the most goals in one season since Ted Drake's total of forty-four in 1935-36 and Henry became an absolute favourite at Highbury.

Wenger knew that he had a team capable of winning the highest honours; he also knew that he had to keep them fired up from the start so that they could deal with Manchester United. In 2000-2001, all that he could do was to keep the Manchester lead down to ten points in a season that began and ended with defeat, 1-0 to Sunderland and 2-3 to Southampton. In between, the Gunners had drowned Manchester City and Newcastle in two 5-0 victories, beaten Manchester United 1-0 at home, thrashed Leicester City 6-1 and been given a 6-1 hiding by Manchester United at Old Trafford. In the FA Cup final, Arsenal had failed against Liverpool and lost 2-1. An eventful year ended, that had been filled with frustration and nothing to show for the tremendous effort except second place in the league. What was the missing ingredient that would turn a superb side into trophy winners? What was needed, suggested Thierry, was a...

..".fox in the box".

THE PASSION & THE GLORY

Unbeknown to anyone, the year in which the *"French Revolution"* would really take off had arrived. Defender Sol Campbell was at Highbury; his move from Tottenham left everyone aghast and some Tottenham fans incensed. He was joining a team that was impressive to say the least, boasting Adams, Bergkamp, Ashley Cole, Lee Dixon, Henry, Ljungberg and Seaman just to name a few.

Wenger wanted the team to come out with all guns blazing, and the 4-0 away win against Middlesborough showed that the team intended to do exactly that. The 1-2 defeat at home to Leeds the next week?

Certainly, that was a slap in the face. The team kept their nerve and wandered up and down the table between first and fourth places until they really got into gear in January 2002. They had been undefeated since a 2-1 away win at Liverpool, their rivals for the championship, in December, but from the 10th of February they won every single match for the rest of the season, thirteen games, flattening Tottenham 2-1 and Manchester United at Old Trafford 1-0. Satisfyingly, that was the game that secured the premiership title for Arsenal. Taking it from the side that had won for three years in a row, the Gunners finished on 87 points, 7 points clear of Liverpool.

The championship success came on the heels of the FA Cup final. Two London clubs were lined up at the Millennium Stadium in Cardiff on May the 4th 2002; Arsenal and Chelsea.

The Gunners kept the fans on tenterhooks for the first half and the teams left the field drawn at 0-0. The second half had been under way for some thirty-five minutes when Ray Parlour took possession of the ball. One Chelsea fan, Tim Lovejoy, was commentating for the Sky Sports Fanzone and said, *"It's alright, it's only Ray Parlour"*. It was alright … for Arsenal, because seconds later a twenty-five-yard shot had put Arsenal in the lead. Just ten minutes later, Ljungberg had performed his magic and curled in the second. Wenger's team had found the magic ingredient at last and picked up their third domestic double to prove it. Henry's flags had been flying high again as he put away thirty-two goals that season.

For Tony Adams, however, it was all over at Arsenal. The 6 ft 4 inch defender, who had spent twenty-two years at the club, one of the greatest Arsenal players of all time with 504 appearances, was going to try his hand at managing, joining Wycombe Wanderers in November 2003.

A double is always a hard act to follow, but Arsenal almost managed to do it in 2002-03. It was a good season, with Brazilian midfielder Gilberto Silva now in the team alongside his fellow countryman Edu. The Community Shield went to the Gunners in August with a 1-0 win against Liverpool to bring confidence to a team that then went on to sink West

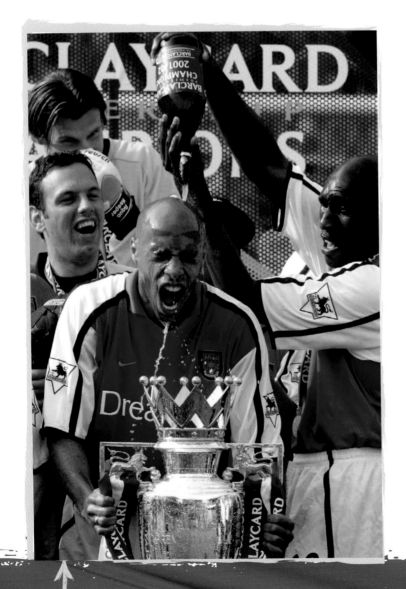

70

Bromwich Albion 5-2 in an undefeated run of nine games. Arsenal were on top of the table for most of the season but fell away in April, and a 2-2 home draw against Manchester United gave the northerners the top spot. There were six losses in total that season, and Manchester United claimed the premiership with 83 points to Arsenal's 78.

Having lost the premiership, all Arsenal eyes were on the FA Cup in May. The team was in the final against Southampton, a side they had beaten soundly 6-1 just ten days before. The match was something of a damp squib, and if the fans were expecting another goal feast they were disappointed. The main thing, as David Seaman pointed out, was that Arsenal lifted the trophy with a 1-0 win, thanks to midfielder Robert Pires.

Two exciting newcomers were in the team for the 2003-04 premiership competition. David Seaman had departed and in his stead came Jens Lehman from German side Borussia Dortmund. Francesc Fàbregas joined the club, too, at just sixteen years of age, in a move from Barcelona. He only made two appearances that season, but both players were part of a side that made league history.

In a reversal of the previous season, all Arsenal eyes were on the premiership competition as the Gunners were pushed out of all the other major trophies, losing in the semi-finals of both the League (3-1 on aggregate to Middlesborough), and FA Cups (1-0 to Manchester United), and the quarter-finals of the UEFA Cup (2-3 on aggregate to Chelsea).

Arsenal fans were to be treated to a unique experience in the

71

The Carling Cup 3rd Round. Nicklas Bendtner takes to the air to score against Newcastle United
25th September 2007

premiership. Henry fired in his 39 goals, Pires hit 19 and Ljungberg 10, amongst others; defenders and midfielders all got in on the act, and the team only failed to score in four games. The Gunners were on top of the table after the second match, a 4-0 away win against Middlesborough, and they held on in first place for most of the season.

They went into the new year unbeaten, and by February, having recovered from a period of four draws in seven matches, were nine points in the lead over Chelsea and back at the top. In a hard-won game at Highbury against Liverpool when they found themselves 2-1 down at half-time, it was Henry who inspired the turn around for the 4-2 victory. A 2-2 draw against Tottenham gave Arsenal the premiership title with not a single game lost. When the season ended with a 2-1 win at home against Leicester, Arsenal were undefeated in all thirty-eight premiership matches, and with 90 points, were 11 points clear of runners-up Chelsea. Twenty-six games had been won, twelve drawn. No club had achieved such a record since Preston North End in 1988-89. Arsenal fans spoke of the 'Invincibles'. Wenger was exhilarated. *"Almost beyond belief"*, was his comment. (Arsenal eventually extended their unbeaten run to 49 games, beating Nottingham Forest's record of 42.)

The 'Invincibles' tag came back to haunt the team as they came down to earth from that extraordinary achievement; all major trophies have escaped them in the intervening eight years. The Gunners bounced between third and fourth in the Premier League every year, reached the semi-finals of the League and FA Cups, and the final of the UEFA Champions League Cup. Bergkamp, Henry, Fàbregas and Silva have gone and been replaced by new stars such as Oliver Giroud, Aaron Ramsey, Jack Wilshere, Lukas Podolski and Theo Walcott.

On the 7th of May 2006, the team played their last game at the revered Highbury ground and moved to the Emirates Stadium, playing their first game there, Dennis Berkamp's testimonial, on the 22nd of July 2006.

At the moment, there is some magnetic attraction between Arsenal and fourth place in the League, it seems. Since Arsène Wenger arrived, Arsenal have rested there six times, but never gone below that and have frequently raised themselves higher.

So, from 2005 until the season of 2013/14, Arsenal were out of the running in every competition. It was the longest period of disappointment since the 1970's, and the closest they ever came to

Carling Cup Semi Final. Cesc Fabregas takes on Spurs 22nd January 2008

73

William Gallas lifts the Emirates Cup after beating Inter Milan 2-1 29th July 2007

the top of the Premiership was third; three times, in fact. If they weren't third then they were fourth. It was enough to make a fan insane; Arsenal obviously had what was needed to get to the top, what was holding them back? Whispers began to circulate and Wenger was the subject of speculation. Robin van Persie whacked in the goals as top goalscorer four times, but to no avail. By the end of the 2011/12 season, van Persie had left the club with no medals for his sterling efforts. Wenger even bought the powerful German forward Lukas Podolski and French striker Olivier Giroud into the team for the new season. Nothing changed. Good football always fell short of expectation.

And then.

Then came the season of 2013/14.

It seemed as though nothing had altered; another famed German footballer, Mesut Özil, came to join the club, and the team started off with a nice 1-3 loss at home to Aston Villa. Oh ye Gods!

And how could a team that won 12 games consecutively in all competitions then go down 6-3 to Manchester City, put four past Coventry, and then lose 5-1 to Liverpool and 6-0 to Chelsea?!

Back to fourth.

Ah, but something, something was now working that had been lacking for all those years of drought.

The results could be seen on the 17th of May 2014 in the FA Cup Final. True, the opposition was *"only"* Hull City, 16th in the table; but the northerners fought like tigers and threatened the Londoners with disaster. The final result, however, ended years of doubt about Arsenal and silverware. The Gunners were capable of getting trophies again. And equally as important they were capable of fighting back.

It was an exciting clash, and despite the shock of being 2-0 down, Arsenal went on to win extra time; and then Aaron Ramsey moved up to the Hull goal on the 109th minute to fire the Gunners to the cup; Arsenal won 3-2. A nine-year trophy drought was over. The relief and joy felt like an hallucinogenic drug.

No one was taking bets on what would happen next, however. everyone was very happy with one signing during the summer; Chilean forward Alexis Sánchez was coming to Arsenal, man that Wenger describes as having power, creativity and much quality". Sánchez did not disappoint and became top goalscorer that very season with 25 goals.

Yet, in the 2014/15 season, Arsenal got off to what can only be described honestly as a sticky start.

With the Community Shield under their belts after a 3-0 victory over Manchester City, hopes had been raised. Which were dashed with just two victories in the first eight Premiership games, at which point they were on sixth position. And by the time they lost to Tottenham Hotspur 1-2 in February 2015, they had gone precisely nowhere. There had been three great consecutive wins culminating in a 5-0 thumping of Aston Villa. By now everyone was resigned to their fate, until, suddenly, the team decided to show what they were made of. The result was ten games undefeated; a run which landed them on third-place, before they inexplicably, and maddeningly, threw away the game at home to Swansea in May, 0-1. Two draws and a win in the final game against West Brom, 4-1, left them adrift on guess where? Yes, third place again. Cosy enough.

However.

Despite the League Cup and the UEFA Cup disappearing over the horizon, the silverware flashed brightly once more.

It was the FA Cup again.

In the run up, Arsenal had gloriously despatched Manchester United away from home, 1-2, with Danny Welbeck delivering the knock-out goal, which meant that they had ditched both Manchester sides in trophy competitions that season. Reading were next to be kicked off the trail, also 2-1, so Arsenal would now make their 28th FA Cup Final appearance.

They ran out against Aston Villa and left them in no doubt who were

Jack Wilshere & Giandomenico Mesto clash in Champions League game 1st October 2013

Alexis Sanchez & David Alaba of Munich battle for the ball during the UEFA Champions League 15 February 2017

the kings of the field that day. Arsenal put on a firecracker display. After 40 minutes, Walcott opened the scoring followed by Alexis Sánchez on 50 minutes scoring one of the FA Cup's unforgettable goals, with a shot just after the half; it was a lightning bolt that swerved and dipped over 25 yards into the goal. Mertesacker came good on the 62nd minute and finally Giroud struck on the 93rd.

It was Arsenal's 12th FA Cup and a cup record. They were also the first team to win by more than one goal since 2004. One in the eye for Wenger's detractors, then, in this two-trophy season.

As though buoyed by that win, Arsenal seemed rejuvenated in the 2015/16 season and were rewarded by their best league placing since the 2004/05 season.

They began with yet another Community Shield win; against arch rivals Chelsea, who they downed 1-0. A very good omen.

So they decided to lose against West Ham at home on the opening match of the season; by 2 goals to 0 even: just to keep fans on their toes, no doubt. Nothing like position 20 to do that, is there?

But they were only kidding and after just two defeats in 16 games they were back to that cosy 3rd position. They lost 7 games in total; but not to the wonder kids from Leicester City, oddly enough In fact they hammered the upstarts 2-5 early in the season and then 2-1 later. They couldn't keep up, though, and ended on 2nd place with 71 points to Leicester's 81. Still, it kept the critics murmurings to a barely audible level.

What is it about those initial games of the season? The Gunners lost at home to Liverpool, 3-4. Ah, but all was soon forgotten because the Gunners in gear produced a superb unbeaten run of 14 games. Chelsea felt the sting with a 3-0 walloping and West Ham received an even bigger hiding; 5-1 to allow Arsenal to go top… where they wavered and lost twice in a row, 1-2 to Everton and Manchester City. Hello 4th place, we know you so well.

In fact, the lads were now on a run that would see them through 14 games without defeat and an absolute goal feast against West Ham in December when Özil opened the scoring after 24 minutes to be followed by that classy man Alexis Sánchez firing on all cylinders, who netted a hat-trick with goals on the 72nd, 80th and 86th minutes, and Oxlade-Chamberlain's superb long shot in the 84th minute. It was a heady win that took the Gunners to second place within earshot of leaders Chelsea, just 3 points ahead.

Then one of the wheels came off the engine.

A defeat by Manchester City, 2-1 in December compounded the damage Everton had done by the same margin the week before, and Arsenal slipped to 5th in the table.

The Gunners came back from that setback and won the next five games, which took them back to 2nd. But Chelsea had extended their lead; 55 points to the Gunner's 47. So there was work to do.

Instead, Arsenal seemed to completely lose heart and entered the doldrums that completely wrecked any hopes of a Premiership title; eight games, just two wins but five defeats. In three of those, to Chelsea, Liverpool and West Brom, Arsenal were sunk 3-1 each time.

And then, of course, there was fearsome February 2017; the UEFA Champions League. Who could forget the two legs, though everyone would like to have the memory surgically removed. It was too awful not to be mentioned here; February: Bayern Munich 5 Arsenal 1. March: Arsenal 1 Bayern Munich 5. With only ten men, it was Arsenal's biggest home defeat since November 1998 and the 5-0 loss to Chelsea in the League Cup.

It would prove impossible to recover from the psychological blows as there was another defeat waiting in the league pipeline which would land them on 6th place.

And then, as though to say, we can if we want to, the team proceeded to belt in two goals against Manchester United one week after the 2-0 defeat at Tottenham. It was the first of five games that ended with the Gunners victorious, as did the 3-1 smacking that Everton received in the last game of the season. The fans also had a brilliant strike in injury-time from Aaron Ramsey, 20 yards out to savour in that game.

Both matches had been a sign of what the team could do; but it was all too late. Wenger's men were in 5th place when the season's whistle finally fell silent. They had missed out on the chance of a Champion's League place for the first time in 20 years.

Alexis Sánchez could be pleased with himself for being voted player of the season and emerging as top goalscorer for the second time in his Arsenal career with 30 goals.

As the league fixtures ended, the seemingly eternal questions about Wenger's future at the club were swirling furiously, fuelled by the manager's own statements. He was not sure if he would still be at Highbury after the FA Cup Final in May, he said.

Perhaps not the best news to send the team out onto the field with in the match against hard opponents Chelsea for the final. The Gunner's season was to begin as it ended; facing Conte's champions.

Arsenal ran out to meet them on the 27th May.

And were ahead after only 4 minutes of play after a flagged offside was dismissed by the referee, and the Gunners were the better side throughout with some outstanding football, and they well deserved Ramsey's winning header in the 79th minute after Diego had equalised for the Blues.

Lifting the cup was proof that Arsenal had more than enough talent to take on and beat the best. The win meant that Arsenal had become the most successful club in FA Cup history, recording a record-breaking thirteenth victory; an extraordinary achievement.

It was also Wenger's seventh FA Cup win, making him the most successful manager in the history of the FA Cup.

Would he now stay at Highbury?

"It's not easy, believe me. I do think I am the right man to do the job. You can't make 35 years at the top level if you believe you're not the right man to do the job", said Wenger, and shortly after the

historic FA Cup victory.

Arsenal can look back with pride on a magnificent history since the meeting in the Royal Oak pub on the 1st of December 1886 that began the life of Dial Square FC. The club has had more than its share of disappointments and trials, but has overcome to them all to rise to triumphant heights. The Gunners have ridden the storms, refused to be downhearted and have consistently dominated the top echelons of English football as no other club has done. With thirteen league championships behind them and Thirteen FA Cups, Arsenal can confidently look forward to the future, and the Arsenal supporters, the 'Gooners', can expect more exciting games filled with the thrilling football for which the Gunners are famous. Some of the most talented players in English football wear, and have worn, Arsenal shirts, and will be succeeded by the stars of the future, to ensure that Arsenal remains one of the greatest clubs in the history of English football.

Arsene Wenger celebrates with midfielder Mohamed Elneny after the Emirates FA Cup Final between Arsenal and Chelsea

81

THE PLAYERS

A list of the most famous players must inevitably be shorter than it should be and will always be disputed by the supporters of one player or another. But here are some of those who must grace every list.

ALEXANDER JAMES

Alexander Wilson James was born in Mossend, Lanarkshire, Scotland on the 14th September 1901 and died on the 1st June 1953. He joined Arsenal from Preston North End in 1929, and was also employed at Selfridges as a 'sports demonstrator', so that the £8 wage limit imposed by the FA could be circumvented.

Inside-forward James has been likened to Dennis Bergkamp. Renowned for his accurate passing and vision, he rose to become an Arsenal star in the Gunners' 1930-31 league title win. Known as 'Wee' Alex because of his size, James was an innovative player; he would weave the ball to the forwards or wingers from a deep position, the first inside-forward to play in that position. His impact on the game can be seen in his performance in the 1932-33 season when it was calculated that he was responsible for more than fifty direct assists. This was where his strength lay rather than in his goal-scoring ability. His confidence and vivacious play meant that he was a favourite with spectators.

His appearance on the field was unmistakable; baggy shorts covered his legs, concealing the long johns that he wore to help keep the acute rheumatism in his ankles at bay. Off the field he was something of a social butterfly and wore dapper suits; he was often seen with famous names of the era.

James retired in 1937 after 231 appearances and 27 goals for the London side.

In WWII, he joined the Royal Artillery, becoming a journalist when the war ended, and then in 1949 he was coach to the Arsenal youth team.

James died at the age of 51 from cancer. In 2005, in recognition of his contribution to the English game, James was inducted into the English Football Hall of Fame.

CLIFF BASTIN

Clifford Sydney Bastin was born on the 14th March 1912 in Heavitree near Exeter, and died on the 4th December 1991.

Alexander James
Cliff Bastin

Bastin joined Arsenal in 1929 when he was just seventeen and remained with them until he retired in 1947, making 395 appearances for the London side. His 178 goals now make up the third highest score for an Arsenal player, a remarkable feat for a left-winger.

Known as 'Boy Bastin' because of his youth, he was noted for his composure under pressure and his deadly accurate shooting, becoming Arsenal's top goalscorer twice, in 1932—33 and in 1933—34. He was also capped for England 21 times, scoring 12 goals for the national side.

Bastin was twenty-seven when WWII began. He was excused military service because of his increasing deafness and served as an ARP Warden. A leg injury that he had sustained in the last game before the war meant that he would play just seven more times once hostilities had finished. He retired and ran a pub in Exeter where he died at the age of seventy-nine.

TED DRAKE

Edward Joseph 'Ted' Drake was born on the 16th August 1912 in Southampton and died on the 30th May 1995.

Drake joined Arsenal in 1934 and ended his playing career with them in 1945 after 184 games and 139 goals.

Courage and skill were the characteristics that marked him out on the field, and with his fierce shooting power and speed, he became Arsenal's top goalscorer for the five seasons from 1934—35 until 1938-39. In December 1935, Drake scored seven goals against Aston Villa, a record for the most goals scored in the top division of the English game.

During World War Two, Drake served in the RAF. A spinal injury sustained shortly after the war forced to him to retire from playing, and he went on to manage several teams, most notably Chelsea.

He died at the age of 82.

TONY ADAMS

Tony Alexander Adams was born on the 10th October 1966 in Romford Dagenham and signed for Arsenal in 1980 when he was still a schoolboy. His first-team debut came on November 5th, 1983 when he was just seventeen years old.

Adams was 6'4" tall, and as a defender he imposed a strong discipline on the Arsenal back line. He became part of the "famous four", which included Steve Bould, Nigel Winterburn and Lee Dixon, and was still only twenty-one years of age when he became club captain on the 1st of January 1988. He remained

Ted Drake
Tony Adams

Thierry Henry

captain until his retirement fourteen years later.

In the mid-1980s, Adams succumbed to alcoholism, which he only confessed to in 1996. It threw his life into turmoil, and he was involved in fights and other alcohol-related problems; at one point he was imprisoned for four months for driving whilst four times over the legal drink-drive limit.

With the encouragement of Arsène Wenger, Adams reformed his life, and he continued to play until 2002 when he retired after a career lasting almost twenty years. With the distinction of being the most successful captain in the club's history, Adams played 669 matches for Arsenal and 66 for the English national side, which he also captained.

George Graham described Adams as *"my colossus"*, and to Arsène Wenger he was a *"professor of defence"*. Excellent leadership qualities, the timing of his tackles and his understanding of the game as well as physical strength, meant that he was a superb defender. At Highbury he was revered by fans.

After leaving Highbury, Adams went to Brunel University to study for a sports science degree. He then became the manager of Wycombe Wanderers in November 2003 and has continued his career as a football manager since then.

In 1987 Adams received the PFA Young Player of the Year award and in 2004 he was awarded an MBE.

THIERRY HENRY

Thierry Daniel Henry was born on the 17th August 1977 in Les Ulis, Essonne, France.

Henry joined Arsenal in 1999, where he was reunited with his former boss at AS Monaco, Arsène Wenger. After a tough first season in which he went nine games without a goal, Henry turned his game around and became a deadly striker feared all over Europe; with 228 goals in all competitions he is Arsenal's all-time leading scorer. He is also the only player to have won the European Golden Boot twice in a row. For four consecutive seasons he was top goal-scorer in the Premier League; 2002, 2004, 2005, 2006.

There are several reasons for his success; he remains calm when challenged or challenging for the ball in front of the goal and has the exceptional speed required to get behind defenders. An unselfish player who thinks creatively, he would frequently be involved in assists after moving temporarily out to the left wing.

One of the high points of his career came in the 2005-2006 season; he was appointed captain, and became the Gunner's top goalscorer of all time on the

17th October 2005. Next, he scored his 100th league goal at Highbury, an achievement unique in Premier League football and in Arsenal's history.

Henry won the FA Cup three times and the League twice at Arsenal, and he has been voted FWA Footballer of the Year, three times as well as being voted best Premier League player of the 2000s.

Henry left Arsenal in 2007 to join Barcelona and then went on to play for the New York Red Bulls.

DENNIS BERGKAMP

Dennis Nicolaas Bergkamp was born on the 10th May 1969, in Amsterdam, Holland.

He came to Highbury in 1995 and like Thierry Henry, Bergkamp only found his rhythm when his first season was well under way, but in his eleven years at Arsenal the Dutchman became one of the legends of the sport, considered to be one of the greatest players of his generation.

He joined Arsenal after two mediocre seasons at Inter Milan and came into his own under Wenger. Playing as a forward behind the main strikers, his forward thinking and attacking attitude created innumerable chances for the forwards.

He has often had to contend with being called a 'dirty player' or a 'cheat', but emphasises that many players want to damage opposing teams mentally and physically and that he needed to counteract that aggression if he was to survive.

His 100th goal for Arsenal came in the 2002-03 season, and he won three premiership titles and four FA Cups with the Gunners.

Bergkamp has won a host of personal awards, including Premier Player of the Year four times; in August 1997, September 1997, March 2002 and February 2004. He was FWA Footballer of the Year in 1997—98 and PFA Players' Player of the Year the same year. In 2007 he was inducted into the English Football Hall of fame, the first Dutch player to be so honoured.

Bergkamp ended his playing career with the Gunners, retiring in 2006, having gained admiration and provided inspiration. He is now in football management.

MARC OVERMARS

Marc Overmars was born on the 29th March 1973 in Emst, Gelderland, Holland. The left-winger joined Arsenal in 1997, despite a serious knee injury

incurred the year before at his previous club, Ajax. Overmars recovered, although as with many players coming to English clubs for the first time, he got off to a slow start. It did not take long for him to prove his worth, with his high-speed runs causing chaos in the opposition defences as he skillfully passed them with the ball or latched onto his team mates' passes. His speed earned him the nickname, *"the Roadrunner"*.

His skill and goalscoring ability helped Arsenal to win the Double in his first season at Highbury. In subsequent seasons, however, Overmars was dogged by injuries and neither he nor Arsenal reached the heights they had attained the previous season. By the summer of 2000 he had joined Spanish club Barcelona.

He played for the Gunners 142 times, putting away 41 goals, many of them at vital points in a game. In the Netherlands, he won 86 caps for the national football team and became Dutch Football Talent of the Year in 1992. He was the Dutch Golden Shoe Winner in 1993 and the FIFA World Cup Best Young Player 1994.

Overmars was, without doubt, one of the finest wingers, not only in Arsenal's history, but in the history of football.

IAN WRIGHT

Ian Edward Wright was born on the 3rd November 1963, in Woolwich, London.

Dennis Bergkamp, Marc Overmars & Ian Wright

off the field, although it was, of course, his skill in front of the goal that made him a legend. His partnership with Dennis Bergkamp remains one of Arsenal's most memorable.

Ending his Arsenal career in 1991, he moved to West Ham United. He is now a soccer coach and well-known media personality. He received an MBE for services to football in the year 2000.

PATRICK VIEIRA

Patrick Vieira was born on the 23rd of June 1976 in Dakar, Senegal. He joined Arsenal in 1996 and had an immediate effect on the team's performance. *"He makes dream passes forward"* said Ian Wright, and the 6'4" midfielder became vital to Wenger's attacking team. It was his grace, coupled with excellent passing skills that made him a firm favourite at Highbury.

The quality of his play and his composure under pressure meant that when Adams retired in 2002 Vieira was chosen to captain the team. The bad behaviour that had characterised his earlier performances now gave way to reveal a mature player, but one who still thrilled the Arsenal fans with control, tackling and awareness skills that were, according to The Guardian, in Vieira's 200th league appearance for Arsenal, *"... exceptional even by his standards".*

Vieira left Arsenal in 2005 after 406 appearances and 33 goals; basically because Wenger wanted to use Fàbregas, and the pairing of the young nineteen-year old with Vieira didn't work.

Vieira joined Italian club Juventus, then moving on to Internazionale and Manchester City. He retired as a player in 2011, to take on a training and youth development role at Manchester City, before becoming manager of the elite development squad in 2013.

Veira is married to Cheryl, who is from Trinidad. Amongst other honours, he was FIFA Confederations Cup Top Scorer in 2001, Premier League Player of the Season 2000—01, French Player of the Year 2001, and he was made a Chevalier of the Legion d'honneur in 1998.

DAVID SEAMAN

David Andrew Seaman was born on the 19th September 1963 in Rotherham, England.

Seaman joined Arsenal in 1990 and remained there as goalkeeper until 2004. Whilst at Arsenal Seaman won three league championships, four FA

Wright joined Arsenal in 1991 and promptly scored a hat-trick on his league debut as he did in his final game of the season, whereupon he was awarded the Golden Boot. For six consecutive seasons, Wright was the Gunners' top goalscorer, eventually ending his Arsenal career with 185 goals in 288 appearances and earning 33 caps with the English national squad.

Wright was known and loved by Arsenal fans for his showmanship on and

Patrick Vieira
David Seaman

cups, the League Cup and the European Cup Winners Cup. He is also the second most capped goalkeeper after Peter Shilton, with 75 caps. His quick reflexes, positional awareness, and courage have meant that he has played in goal for Arsenal more than any other keeper, having appeared for the club 564 times. He is now a goalkeeping coach.

The save that will live in the memory of everyone who saw it came in April 2003. Arsenal were nursing a 1-0 lead against Sheffield United in the FA Cup semi-final at Old Trafford. With less than ten minutes to go and with Seaman adrift at the far post, Paul Peschisolido headed the ball at the Arsenal net. The keeper threw himself sideways and backwards to drag the ball away from his goal.

Seaman went on to captain the side that won the FA Cup that year, in his last match for the Gunners.

He received the Premier League 10 Seasons Award in 1992-2002 as part of the Domestic Team of the Decade, and as Goalkeeper with the Most Clean Sheets; 130, including 23 clean sheets in the 1990—91 season when Arsenal won the league.

CHARLIE GEORGE

Charles Frederick 'Charlie' George was born on the 10th October 1950 in Islington, England. He joined Arsenal in 1966 making his debut for the club on the 9th August 1969.

The highlight of his career came in the 1970—71 season. Having broken his ankle at the start of the season, he returned to help Arsenal claim the league title and then, with a spectacular twenty-yard shot that scored the winning goal, the FA Cup.

Although his confidence and ball skills made him a favourite with the fans at Highbury, his time at Arsenal was pitted with rebellious behaviour and injuries, and his form declined along with Arsenal's fortunes; in the 1974—75 season he was dropped from the first team after an argument with manager Bertie Mee. In 1975 he moved to Derby County having played 179 times for Arsenal and scored 49 goals. He retired in 1983. He is now a match day host at Arsenal.

MESUT ÖZIL

Mesut Özil was born on the 15th of October 1988 in Gelsenkirchen, Germany.

Charlie George
Mesut Özil.

The 1.80m (5ft 11in) Özil, An attacking midfielder, has played for several of Germany's top clubs; Shalke 04, Bayer Leverkusen and Bayern Munich. His talents was sought after by many of Europe's premier clubs, and after a spell at Werder Bremen he joined the Spanish club Real Madrid in 2010 where he stayed for the next three seasons and was no stranger to standing ovations in the stadia in which he played and praise for his performances.

In 2013, Özil moved across the English Channel to London and joined Arsenal on a five-year deal. When he did so, he became the most expensive German footballer in the history of the game.

And he did not disappoint. If he could not play because of injury, he was sorely missed.

Özil had been highly praised for his sophisticated playing skill and creative thinking on the ball. His reading of a game is second to none and enables him to break open a tight situation. Thanks to his stylish skill in providing assists for his team-mates on the flanks or as a winger, Özil has been compared to a legendary Real Madrid player; Zinedine Zidane. The praise came from none other than José Mourinho, who also described him as *"unique"*. *The media simply call him, the "Assist King"*, a well-deserved accolade as he has more assists than any other player in the history of the Premiership game.

As of summer 2017, Özil has scored 23 goals for Arsenal and 21 for the German national squad.

OLIVIER GIROUD

Olivier Giroud was born on the 30th of September 1986 in Chambéry, France. His senior career began in 2005 with Grenoble, having spent six years training with his home club, Froges and he remained with French teams — Istres, Tours, Montpellier — until joining Arsenal in 2012; now a player sought after by many other clubs.

He was soon putting home the goals and became top goalscorer in the 2013/14 season with 22 and again in the 2015/16 season with 24 goals. Since arriving at Arsenal, he has netted 69 goals in all competitions.

Valued for his consistency in scoring goals, his size and strength have proven invaluable up front, as has his accuracy in heading and his powerful shooting. Giroud also acts as a pivotal link man.

The 1.92m (6ft 4in) striker has earned more than 50 caps for the French international team.

Giroud has garnered a host of personal awards:

- **The UNFP Ligue 2 Player of the Year for 2009/10.**
- **The Ligue 2 top goalscorer for 2009/10.**
- **The UNFP Ligue 2 Team of the Year for 2009/10.**
- **The Ligue 2 UNFP Player of the Month in Sept 2009 and Nov 2009.**
- **The Ligue 1 top goalscorer for 2011/12.**
- **The UNFP Ligue 1 Team of the Year for 2011/12.**
- **The Premier League Player of the Month in March 2015.**
- **The UEFA European Championship Bronze Boots in 2016.**
- **On a lighter note, in February 2015, Giroud won the vote for the 'Hottest Premier League Player'.**

Olivier Giroud

ALEXIS ALEJANDRO SÁNCHEZ SÁNCHEZ

Alexis Alejandro Sánchez Sánchez was born on the 19th of December 1988 in Tocopilla, Chile.

After making his debut with Cobreloa in 2005, the 1 69m (5ft 6 1/2inch) Sánchez's talents brought him to the Chilean international team in 2006, where he has become the team's second most capped player, and then to Barcelona in 2011; his £25 million pounds signing made him the most expensive transfer in the history of Chilean football.

He was dogged by injuries during his first season but began to find his form during the 2012/13 season. And the goals continued to flow in the following season, which he ended with 21 added to his tally, his highest number to that date.

Wenger brought the young player to Arsenal in time for the 2014/15 season. There, he enjoyed an early shower of compliments, and he soon began to justify Wenger's faith in him. His skills brought him 25 goals to make him the season's leading goalscorer, the final goal having been scored at the 2015 FA Cup Final. He became top goalscorer again the 2016/17 season with

30 goals, scoring in Arsenal's FA Cup final win.

Sometimes called simply Alexis, Sánchez is a multifaceted player who can be used in a variety of roles on the flanks and in the centre of the field as a main striker, a winger or attacking midfielder. His technical abilities are magical, and he possesses the ability to use either foot, incredible speed, is a master of the feint, and is a generous player, who will feed his teammates goalscoring opportunities.

Although still such a young player, he has received many personal awards:

- **The PFA Fans' Player of the Year for 2015.**
- **The Football Supporters' Federation Player of the Year for 2015.**
- **The Facebook FA Premier League Player of the Year in 2015.**
- **The Kids' Choice Awards Favourite UK Footballer in 2015.**
- **The Arsenal Player of the Season for 2014/15.**
- **The Premier League PFA Team of the Year for 2014/15.**
- **The Copa América Golden Ball for 2016.**
- **The Copa América Team of the Tournament: 2016**
- **Serie A Player of the Month in February 2011.**
- **The PFA Fans' Player of the Month in October 2014 and October 2015.**
- **Arsenal Player of the Season 2016/17.**

Alexis Alejandro Sánchez

THE MANAGERS

A brief list of Arsenal managers

HERBERT CHAPMAN

Herbert Chapman was born on the 19th January 1878 in Kiveton Park near Rotherham and died on the 6th January 1934. He was one of eleven children, but unlike his father John he did not go down into the mines but won a place at Sheffield Technical College. As an adult, his football career began when he started to play for Ashton North End in 1895, and continued from then until 1909 when his career as a player ended at Northampton Town where he had been player-manager since 1907.

Chapman joined Arsenal in 1925 and immediately set about changing the Arsenal side. The offside law had been changed that year, and making full use of an idea put forward by thirty-four-year-old Charlie Buchan, who had just signed for the club, Chapman introduced a 3—4—3 formation. This, combined with his own emphasis on strong defence, fast wingers and swift, counter-attacking football, was to be the hallmark of his period as manager.

In 1926, Chapman was involved in a scandal that concerned secret illegal payments made by Arsenal to Charlie Buchan. Chapman was not punished, but club chairman Sir Henry Norris was banned from football, and Chapman's power and influence at Arsenal increased.

Chapman's five-year plan paid dividends in 1930 when Arsenal won the 1930 FA Cup final, their first major trophy. The manager would eventually see his team win the League in the 1930-31 season, with a record-breaking 66 points, and again in 1932-33. Arsenal won the League again in the 1933-34, but by that time Chapman had passed away.

Chapman is known as 'the great innovator', and managers all over the world took up his ideas about how the game should be played. He introduced swift, counter- attacking football which was in great contrast to the way football had been played in England up until then. He was also one of the first managers to take full responsibility for the team, choosing the players himself rather than leaving this to the board members. Chapman believed that physical fitness was very important and he introduced a training regime which included the use of masseurs and physiotherapists. At the weekly team meetings that he instituted, he encouraged his players to discuss tactics.

Chapman was involved in all aspects of the game; he designed the

Herbert Chapman
George Allison

scoreboard and turnstiles at Highbury, oversaw the building of the West Stand, and was even instrumental in having the London Underground station 'Gillespie Road' renamed 'Arsenal'. In 1930, both teams walked out together at the FA Cup final; this was the first time it had happened and was due to Chapman's involvement with both teams, Arsenal and Huddersfield Town.

In January 1934 Chapman caught a cold which quickly turned into pneumonia. Early on the morning of January 6th, 1934 he died at the age of 55 at his home in London.

GEORGE ALLISON

George Frederick Allison was born on the 24th October 1883 in Darlington and died on the 13th March 1957. He worked as a newspaper and radio sports journalist and joined Arsenal as club secretary and then managing director before taking up the role of team manager in 1934. He became the club's second longest-serving manager, staying with the club for thirteen years.

Unlike Herbert Chapman, Allison did not take responsibility for training and discipline, leaving this to his assistants Joe Shaw and Tom Whittaker. Although criticised for his lack of a deep understanding of the game, he was described as tactful and good-hearted. Whilst in charge at Arsenal, Allison saw the Gunners win their third league title, in 1934-35, and then the FA Cup in 1936. Under his leadership, they won the league title again in 1938.

After the Second World War had finished, many of Arsenal's top players had retired from the game, and Allison decided that he no longer wished to continue as a manager. He retired in 1947, and died ten years later in 1957 after a long period of illness.

BERTIE MEE

Bertie Mee was born in Nottinghamshire on December 25th 1918 and died on the 22nd October 2001.

When Billy Wright was sacked in 1966, Mee was chosen to become the new Arsenal manager at a time when the club were putting in mediocre performances. He had joined Arsenal in 1960 as a physiotherapist, and in order to make up for his lack of tactical and coaching knowledge, he chose Dave Sexton and Don Howe as his assistants. Mee's strong points were discipline and attention to detail; armed with these, he helped Arsenal to become one of the top teams in Europe.

He revitalised the Arsenal team with young players, and in 1970 his Arsenal team brought home their first trophy for seventeen years; the Fairs Cup.

He achieved even greater success the following season when Arsenal won the league and cup double, only the second team to achieve this in the 20th century.

This proved to be the peak of his career. Mee was accused of dismantling the team that had won the Double, and indeed, Arsenal were never to achieve such heights under his leadership again.

Mee left Arsenal in 1976 to join Watford where he took on a variety of roles. In 1984 he was awarded an OBE for his services to football.

Bertie Mee died at the age of 82, but he remains a favourite at Arsenal for helping the club back to winning form.

Bertie Mee

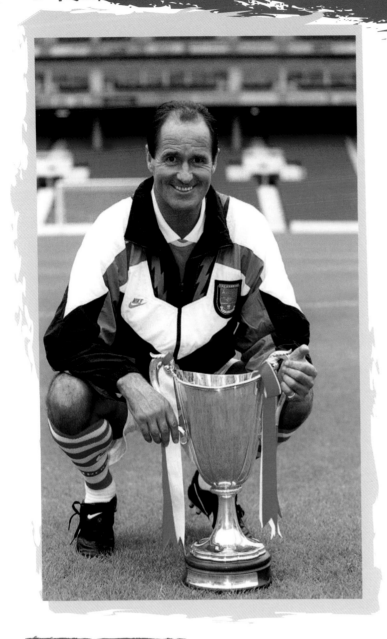

signing many players who became stars at Arsenal such as Tony Adams, David Seaman, Ian Wright, Lee Dixon and Anders Limpar.

In 1987, his revitalised team went on to win the League Cup. In 1989, Graham's third season in charge, Arsenal went on to finish top of Division One, the first time they had done so since 1971, and he helped them win the title again in 1991.

When the club competed for the European Cup for the first time in twenty years, Graham was still in charge. In 1992-93, Graham's Arsenal achieved the FA Cup and League Cup double, following this the next season by winning the UEFA Cup Winners Cup. In 1994 he added the Cup Winners Cup to his list of trophies.

Sadly, Graham was found to have received an illegal payment of £425,000 from a Norwegian agent and was dismissed from his job in 1995.

He will be remembered at Arsenal for his uncompromising attitude, which he passed on to his players, for building one of the tightest defences in the League, his ability to spot talented players and for being responsible for one of the most successful periods in Arsenal's history.

Graham went on to manage Leeds United Tottenham Hotspur and is now a football commentator on Sky Sports.

ARSÈNE WENGER

Arsène Wenger was born in Strasbourg, Alsace, Eastern France on the 22nd of October 1949. His mother's name was Louise and his father, Alphonse, was the manager of the local village football team, and introduced his son to the game when Arsène was six years old. The young boy went to Lemnos primary school, and the family ran a bistro, La Croix d'Or, as well as a business supplying spare parts for cars. Arsène's parents wanted their son to enter the family business when he left school.

Arsène spent his childhood in the village of Duttlenheim and only learned to speak French when he was 7, having spoken the local Germanic dialect up until then. He played for the village football team — whose HQ was in the family bistro — when he was 12, but he was often taken by his father across the border to Germany to watch matches. As he grew older he organised the Duttlenheim team's matches.

When he was 18, Wenger junior was good enough to be recruited by Mutzig of the French Third Division, renowned as being the best amateur club in Alsace. Despite what has been described as a 'modest' career as a

GEORGE GRAHAM

George Graham was born on the 30th November 1944 in Bargeddie near Coatbridge in Scotland.

Graham signed to play for Arsenal in 1966 and had a successful career there, leaving to join Manchester United in 1972. He returned to Arsenal as the team's manager in May 1986 at a time when Arsenal were beginning to lose contact with the top teams in the League, and many observers credit him with laying the foundations for the team's future successes. Graham immediately set about bringing younger players into the team and improving discipline, which brought immediate results. Graham was responsible for

George Graham

player, Wenger was engaged as a defender by several other clubs, starting with Mulhouse, joining that team in 1973, and appearing for them fifty-six times.

Wenger wanted to live and breathe football, but his parents insisted that he continue his studies, so he went to the Institut Européen d'Etudes Commerciales Supérieures de Strasbourg of the Robert Schuman University; he gained his masters' degree in economics there in 1974. He also improved his English with a course in Cambridge, England.

He kept on playing football, and in 1975 moved on to ASPV Strasbourg before turning professional in 1978 with RC Strasbourg. Although he only played for the club on twelve occasions he did manage to play in the UEFA Cup.

Wenger now had his eye on a managerial role, and by 1981 had a manager's diploma in his pocket and became coach for the Strasbourg club's youth team.

In 1983, he was ready for greater things and moved on to AS Cannes in Division Two, where he took the job as assistant manager. One year later, he was on the move again, this time to First Division Nancy and his first full

managerial position.

With no money to spend, and after three seasons there — in which the club came in 12th, 18th and 19th, and were then relegated — Wenger resigned. It seemed that his talents were already apparent, because he had attracted the interest of FC Monaco and joined the club in 1987.

Monaco were right to trust the young man; Wenger guided the club to the league title that year with a six-point lead. The next season they were third but reached the final of the Coupe de France losing to Marseille, 4-3 who they beat the following year in the final. In the League they were again third.

Wenger was forced to stay on at Monaco despite interest from Bayern Munich, and he became increasingly disillusioned with corruption in the football business his home country. Monaco dismissed him in September 1994 and he left France for Japan joining Nagoya Grampus Eight. Again Wenger showed that he was a force to be reckoned with; his club won the Emperors' Cup, and the team were then runners-up in the League in his second season. He was awarded the title of League Manager of the Year in 1995.

Wenger's great chance came in 1996 when Bruce Rioch was dismissed from London club, Arsenal. On the 30th of September, Wenger was officially the new manager. Hardly anyone had heard of the new man; *"Arsène Who?"*, howled the London Evening Standard after his appointment became public.

Even before starting work, Wenger had told the club that they should buy Patrick Vieira and Rémi Garde, and he maintains to this day that Vieira was the best acquisition of his career at Arsenal.

Wenger's skills brought the Gunners third place in May 1997, but the manager stunned everyone by helping Arsenal to win the Double the following year; the Premier League and the FA Cup.

1997 was also the year that his wife, Annie Brosterhous, a former basketball player, gave birth to the couple's daughter, Léa.

Now the club's longest-serving manager, he is also the most successful, helping Arsenal to win eleven trophies since 1996.

So far he has won the Premiership three times, the FA Cup four times, (which includes the League and FA Cup double, twice), and the Charity Shield four times. In the 2003-04 season, the team was undefeated, the first team in 115 years to achieve this record. They went on to forty-nine games without defeat beating the forty-two-match record set by Nottingham Forest.

Wenger's philosophy is to encourage young talent and bring in experienced players who do not command the highest fees but whom he can mould into winning performers; Arsenal stars such as Dennis Bergkamp, Marc Overmars, Nicolas Anelka and Thierry Henry arrived at Highbury thanks to this way of thinking. Here is one example of what can be achieved in this manner; en route to the UEFA Champions League final against Barcelona in 2005-06, the defence that cost Arsenal less than £5m to assemble, set a new record by not conceding a single goal in ten consecutive games.

As always, Wenger has an eye to building a team that can play entertaining, attack-oriented football; Patrick Vieira, Francesc Fàbregas, Robin Van Persie and Kolo Touré, are just some of the relatively unknown players that Wenger assisted to world-class form and fame. Arsenal's manager encapsulated his own philosophy very succinctly when he said, *"We do not buy superstars. We make them"*.

Football experts credit 'Le Professeur' — Wenger's nickname on account of his serious nature — for helping to revolutionise English football in the 1990s, and his presence in the UK has, indeed, had a tremendous impact on the football world. He altered his players' training methods and paid close attention to their diets, banishing the junk food that had served as meals for many of the players until then.

"What's really dreadful is the diet in Britain", Wenger complained. *"The whole day you drink tea with milk and coffee with milk and cakes. If you had a fantasy world of what you shouldn't eat in sport, it's what you eat here"*.

Despite his measured performances in interviews, Wenger also has a ruthless streak that he brings out if he believes that it serves the team's success. Yet he will stand resolutely by his men when they prove to be human, as did by Tony Adams when he was struggling with alcoholism. Wenger's steadfastness enabled Adams to return to first-class fitness.

That Wenger's loyalty to his team knows few boundaries can be seen from this quote;

"Sometimes I see it (a foul by an Arsenal player), but I say that I didn't see it to protect the players and because I could not find any rational explanation for what they did".

And Wenger's fairness was not in doubt when he offered Sheffield Wednesday a replay match after a misunderstanding that led to a 2-1 Arsenal victory.

The manager is no stranger to controversy, however. He is not averse to launching attacks at officials if he feels wronged by decisions. On one infamous occasion he called a linesman a liar, which brought an FA investigation down on his head and a fine of £2500. Jose Mourinho felt the lash of his tongue, too, after the Chelsea manager had complained that Wenger was obsessed with 'the Blues'.

"He's out of order, disconnected with reality and disrespectful", said Wenger. *"When you give success to stupid people, it makes them more stupid sometimes and not more intelligent"*.

He even admits to avoiding awkward press questions by being less than liberal with the truth.

It is, perhaps, a result of Wenger considering himself a citizen of the world that Arsenal has employed so many foreign players, one feature of the club that has led to criticism in many circles. (Wenger speaks three languages fluently, French, English and German, and also speaks some Spanish, Italian and Japanese; he has been awarded the French Legion D'Honneur and an honorary OBE in the UK, and the Freedom of the Borough of Islington, London, UK.) Wenger is unrepentant. *"Values and qualities are important"*, is his answer to those who bemoan the lack of English players in his teams. Passports, in his eyes, are not.

Whatever his faults, Arsène Wenger's exceptional managerial ability has

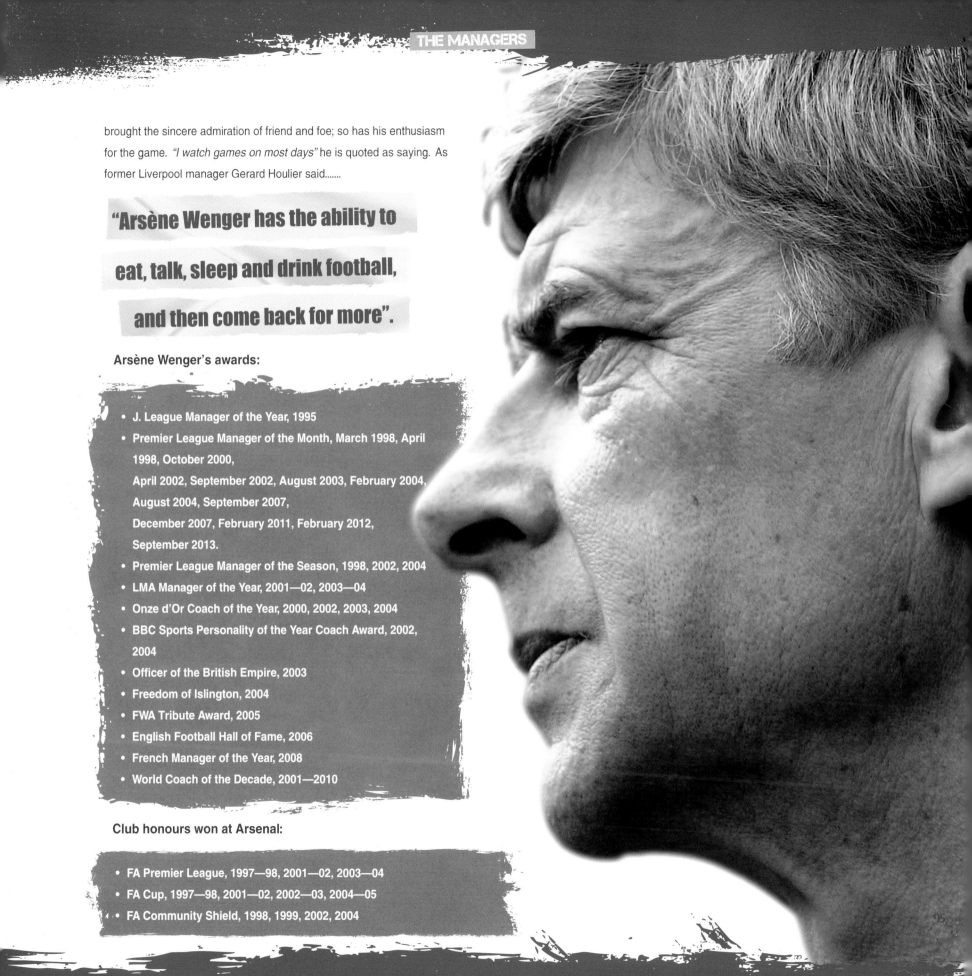

brought the sincere admiration of friend and foe; so has his enthusiasm for the game. *"I watch games on most days"* he is quoted as saying. As former Liverpool manager Gerard Houlier said.......

"Arsène Wenger has the ability to eat, talk, sleep and drink football, and then come back for more".

Arsène Wenger's awards:

- J. League Manager of the Year, 1995
- Premier League Manager of the Month, March 1998, April 1998, October 2000,
  April 2002, September 2002, August 2003, February 2004, August 2004, September 2007,
  December 2007, February 2011, February 2012, September 2013.
- Premier League Manager of the Season, 1998, 2002, 2004
- LMA Manager of the Year, 2001—02, 2003—04
- Onze d'Or Coach of the Year, 2000, 2002, 2003, 2004
- BBC Sports Personality of the Year Coach Award, 2002, 2004
- Officer of the British Empire, 2003
- Freedom of Islington, 2004
- FWA Tribute Award, 2005
- English Football Hall of Fame, 2006
- French Manager of the Year, 2008
- World Coach of the Decade, 2001—2010

Club honours won at Arsenal:

- FA Premier League, 1997—98, 2001—02, 2003—04
- FA Cup, 1997—98, 2001—02, 2002—03, 2004—05
- FA Community Shield, 1998, 1999, 2002, 2004

THE STATISTICS

POSITION IN THE LEAGUE:

DIVISION TWO
1893/94 - 9
1894/95 - 8
1895/96 - 7
1896/97 - 10
1897/98 - 5
1898/99 - 7
1899/1900 - 8
1900/01 - 7
1901/02 - 4
1902/03 - 3
1903/04 - 2

DIVISION ONE
1904/05 - 10
1905/06 - 12
1906/07 - 7
1907/08 - 14

1908/09 - 6
1909/10 - 18
1910/11 - 10
1911/12 - 10
1912/13 - 20

DIVISION TWO
1913/14 - 3
1914/15 - 5

WORLD WAR

DIVISION ONE
1919/20 - 10
1920/21 - 9
1921/22 - 7
1922/23 - 11
1923/24 - 19
1924/25 - 20

1925/26 - 2
1926/27 - 11
1927/28 - 10
1928/29 - 9
1929/30 - 14
1930/31 - 1
1931/32 - 2
1932/33 - 1
1933/34 - 1
1934/35 - 1
1935/36 - 6
1936/37 - 3
1937/38 - 1
1938/39 - 5
1939/40 - 3

WORLD WAR II

1946/47 - 13
1947/48 - 1
1948/49 - 5
1949/50 - 6
1950/51 - 5
1951/52 - 3
1952/53 - 1
1953/54 - 12
1954/55 - 9
1955/56 - 5
1956/57 - 5
1957/58 - 12
1958/59 - 3
1959/60 - 13
1960/61 - 11
1961/62 - 10
1962/63 - 7
1963/64 - 8

1964/65 - 13
1965/66 - 14
1966/67 - 7
1967/68 - 9
1968/69 - 4
1969/70 - 12
1970/71 - 1
1971/72 - 5
1972/73 - 2
1973/74 - 10
1974/75 - 16
1975/76 - 7
1976/77 - 8
1977/78 - 5
1978/79 - 7
1979/80 - 4
1980/81 - 3
1981/82 - 4

1982/83 -10
1983/84 - 6
1984/85 - 7
1985/86 - 7
1986/87 - 4
1987/88 - 6
1988/89 - 1
1989/90 - 4
1990/91 - 1
1991/92 - 4

PREMIER LEAGUE
1992/93 - 10
1993/94 - 4
1994/95 - 12
1995/96 - 5
1996/97 - 3
1997/98 - 1

1998/99 - 2
1999/2000 - 2
2000/01 - 2
2001/02 - 1
2002/03 - 2
2003/04 - 1
2004/05 - 2
2005/06 - 4
2006/07 - 4
2007/08 - 3
2008/09 - 4
2009/10 - 3
2010/11 - 4
2011/12 - 3
2012/13 - 4
2014/15 - 3
2015/16 - 2
2016/17 - 5

FA PREMIERSHIP/FIRST DIVISION LEAGUE TITLES:

1930/31 - 66 points
1932/33 - 58 points
1933/34 - 59 points
1934/35 - 58 points
1937/38 - 52 points
1947/48 - 59 points
1952/53 - 54 points
1970/71 - 65 points
1988/89 - 76 points
1990/91 - 83 points
1997/98 - 78 points
2001/02 - 87 points
2003/04 - 90 points

CUP COMPETITIONS

FA CUP
1930 - Arsenal 2-0 Huddersfield
1936 - Arsenal 1-0 Sheffield United
1950 - Arsenal 2-0 Liverpool
1971 - Arsenal 2-0 Liverpool
1979 - Arsenal 3-2 Manchester United
1993 - Arsenal 1-1 Sheffield Wednesday
Arsenal 2-1 Sheffield Wednesday (Replay)
1998 - Arsenal 2-0 Newcastle United
2002 - Arsenal 2-0 Chelsea
2003 - Arsenal 1-0 Southampton
2005 - Arsenal 0-0 Manchester United
(Arsenal won on penalties)
2014 - Arsenal 3-2 Hull City
2015 - Arsenal 4-0 Aston Villa
2017 - Arsenal 2-1 Chelsea

FA CHARITY SHIELD
1930 - Arsenal 2-1 Sheffield Wednesday
1931 - Arsenal 1-0 West Bromwich Albion
1934 - Arsenal 4-0 Manchester City
1935 - Arsenal 3-0 Everton
1938 - Arsenal 2-1 Preston North End
1948 - Arsenal 4-3 Manchester United
1953 - Arsenal 3-1 Blackpool
1991 - Arsenal 0-0 Tottenham Hotspur
1998 - Arsenal 3-0 Manchester United
1999 - Arsenal 2-1 Manchester United
2014 - Arsenal 3-0 Manchester City
2015 - Arsenal 1-0 Chelsea

INTER-CITIES FAIRS CUP
1970 - Arsenal 1-3 Anderlecht
Arsenal 3-0 Anderlecht (Second leg

FA LEAGUE CUP
1993 - Arsenal 2-1 Sheffield Wednesday
1987 - Arsenal 2-1 Liverpool

MERCANTILE CREDIT CENTENARY TROPHY
1998-1999 - Arsenal 2-1 Manchester United

FA COMMUNITY SHIELD
2002 - Arsenal 1-0 Liverpool
2004 - Arsenal 3-1 Manchester United